What so
MI

MW01064970

This book is a call for state legislatures around the country to fulfill their responsibility to restructure health care.

—Assistance Majority Leader Bruce W. Bannister
SC House of Representatives

Misdiagnosed shows patient safety activists how to unite under one big tent to make greater patient safety happen in every hospital and surgery center.

—Dianne Parker, Founder of Advocates
in Action for Patient Safety and
2009 Lewis W. Blackmon Patient Safety
Champion Award winner in the advocate's category.

In his new book, *Misdiagnosed!*, Dr. Ira Williams asks a legitimate question: How can we improve health care without first understanding its organizational structure? His notion that Individual Responsibility Peer Review (IRPR) can and should replace the current medical malpractice system for assuring quality is laid out in a convincing manner. As an obstetrician and expert witness, I applaud Dr. Williams for thinking outside the box in this very readable treatise.

—Margaret M. Thompson, MD, JD, MPAff, Adjunct
Professor, The LBJ School of Public Affairs,
The University of Texas

MISDIAGNOSED!

Why Current Health Care
Change is Malpractice

MISDIAGNOSED!

Dr. Ira E. Williams

Author of *First, Do No Harm*
The Cure for Medical Malpractice

TATE PUBLISHING & *Enterprises*

Published by Tate Publishing & Enterprises, LLC
127 E. Trade Center Terrace | Mustang, Oklahoma 73064 USA
1.888.361.9473 | www.tatepublishing.com

Tate Publishing is committed to excellence in the publishing industry. The company reflects the philosophy established by the founders, based on Psalm 68:11,
"The Lord gave the word and great was the company of those who published it."

Book design copyright © 2010 by Tate Publishing, LLC. All rights reserved.
Cover design by Tyler Evans
Interior design by Stephanie Woloszyn

Published in the United States of America

ISBN: 978-1-61566-951-6
Medical / Health Policy
10.03.12

Dedication

To the thousands of "never events" who constitute the
dark side of the quality of health care and to their loved ones,
the collateral damage left to pick up the pieces, because
medical malpractice litigation was chosen to be the system
of choice for the review of questionable patient care.

TABLE OF CONTENTS

INTRODUCTION.. 11

COMPONENTS OF HEALTH CARE..................... 17
    Major Components... 17
    Minor Components... 32

WHAT WENT WRONG? 45
    Major Components... 45
    Minor Components... 62

WHAT WENT RIGHT? 97

HOW TO FIX IT... 113

OTHER OFFERINGS 157

PERSONAL PERSPECTIVE 179

TALES FROM THE DARK SIDE 187

SUMMARY 205

A CHALLENGE.. 209

APPENDIX A 211

APPENDIX B 213

APPENDIX C 245

APPENDIX D 251

END NOTES.. 255

INTRODUCTION

"If you could, what would you change?"

"Wrong question!"

That exchange occurred some months ago between my South Carolina state representative and me regarding our current health care system and its many problems.

Everyone talks of "changing health care," when no one with any potential to participate in that worthy endeavor has the slightest idea how to describe, in detail, our health care system's current organizational structure.

Hubris is defined as excessive pride or self-confidence, and appears to be a strong characteristic of all persons dealing with health care in general and health care change in particular.

President Jimmy Carter and the Democratic Congress took the E out of HEW and created the Department of Education in 1980. That department's 2007 budget was seventy-one billion dollars; therefore, over the past twenty-eight years and countless billions of dollars, what is the current status of education in America today? People seeking instant health care change are shouting for those same people, Congress, to now "work their magic" on our health care system. *Hubris trumps Logic!*

The correct question regarding health care change requires two parts. Can anyone:

a. Describe that entire system, in detail, as to its organizational structure?

b. Describe the process each component took to contribute to its present configuration?

I can and will.

The failed Clinton attempt to change health care fifteen years ago and all current calls for change focus primarily on cost and access—both very important aspects of health care and where society feels much of its pain. However, anyone who believes cost and access health care change will solve even much of the true problems of our current health care system is delusional.

The Minneapolis bridge tragedy, a very sensitive subject, is the perfect analogy of what is wrong with our health care system. Repairs were being made on visual defects when that bridge's infrastructure collapsed.

This book will describe the organizational structure of health care, how that current system came to be, and more prudent steps for future health care change. Health care in America is in chaos, and partisan political efforts based upon half-truths will only make matters worse. The simple fact that no one can name a single aspect of our current health care system that is free of problem *should* demand far more thorough understanding of the entire system prior to any attempt in "changing" that system.

Caveat

Clinton's attempt to change health care fifteen years ago focused primarily on the cost and access aspects of our health care system. Almost all current discussions, books, and political exhortations regarding our health care problems also focus primarily on the cost and access aspects of that system.

Health care cost and access concerns are exceedingly important and deserve such attention, but cost and access health care change—alone—can never make things right in our nation's health care system.

One premise of this book is to advance the understanding that future discussions and debates regarding health care change would greatly benefit from dividing the subject matter into two separate categories, organizational infrastructure, and cost and access. Quality of care and cost of care, understandably, cannot be separated. However, commingling how to fund health care with how to administer its delivery creates an enormously convoluted subject too vast for human comprehension.

One central purpose of this book is to demonstrate the benefits of such a separation of subject matter. A reader will finally be able to say, "I have discovered our health care system's organizational infrastructure, and it can no longer hide."

Enigma of Health Care

Health care cost and access are the primary targets for all current plans to *change* that system.

But—Cost and access can *never* be controlled without better control of quality of medicine (defensive medicine)

But—Quality of medicine is a *function* of the administration of healthcare

But—Administration of health care is a *function* of the organizational structure of health care

But—No one can describe the organizational structure of health care, the system everyone is seeking to change.

The resultant *enigma* of health care continues to be ignored by those seeking to change that system.

Therefore, how much should you trust someone who says, "I know you have a big problem, and I can fix that problem for you. I can't describe all of the details of your problem, but trust me, I know I can finally fix your problem, even though I have been a big part of that problem."

You are soon going to find out how much you

can trust such a person(s), because *someone* is going to start changing your health care system—*soon!* And that is the same person(s) who have, for many years, been contributing to the problem.

Today is the first day of the rest of your life! At some point between today and your last day (everyone is guaranteed a last day), you will come face-to-face with *your health care system* while wearing a flimsy gown that ties in the front for women and in the back for men.

This book is about *your* health care system, and change is coming to that system, even though not all change makes things better. The question that should be asked is, Will *your* health care system be there for you when *you* need it?

A far different approach to understanding the workings of *your health care system* is presented in the following manner:

CHAPTER 1 *(Components of Health Care)* recognizes the major and minor components of health care and offers a working model of that system's organizational infrastructure.

CHAPTER 2 *(What Went Wrong?)* provides examples of how each of the six health care components has contributed, each in their own way, to the present state of health care confusion.

CHAPTER 3 *(What Went Right?)* illustrates three examples of positive health care events that have been mislabeled in the case of the first and recklessly ignored in the case of the other two.

CHAPTER 4 *(How to Fix It?)* offers three recommendations for including a system of medical peer review that, if utilized properly, will allow doctors to fairly judge the questionable patient care of other doctors without attorneys, courts, and juries.

CHAPTER 5 *(Other Offerings)* discusses two highly contentious attempts at dealing with medical malpractice and two relatively new efforts in the never-ending pursuit for better patient safety.

CHAPTER 6 *(Personal Perspective)* is the author's privilege of *blowing off steam* that too many will confuse as anger, when it is really the effects of decades of frustration.

CHAPTER 7 *(Tales From the Dark Side)* attempts to allow the reader to visualize *never events* from the perspective of a medically harmed patient.

COMPONENTS OF HEALTH CARE

Major Components: Organized Medicine

Doctors—Health care began with a basic unit of one doctor and one patient, and that basic unit remains the foundational element of health care today. Most of the history of health care involves doctors of widely varying levels of medical knowledge treating patients as best as they could. Much later, groups of doctors began to concentrate on patient care, when possible, in so-called "hospitals." Finally, very late in the history of health care, governmental attempts at health care regulation began to dramatically alter the health care landscape.

This latter, most recent health care development has, in many respects, transformed the original doctor-patient relationship into a tripartite arrangement, with inevitably conflicting purposes. Two separate forces, one within the medical profession and the other outside, rapidly changed the fundamentals of health care too fast for human comprehension.

America began her national existence with an estimated 3,500 doctors, but unfortunately, Dr. Benjamin Rush, a signer of the Declaration of Independence, was one of the 10 percent minority of doctors who actually possessed a medical degree. However, regardless of the extreme variance of medical expertise found within the medical profession at any given time in its history, doctors ruled health care in America until that recent twin collision with uncontrollable forces from within the profession and without.

Organized medicine was represented solely by the founding of the American Medical Association (AMA) in 1847, followed by the American College of Surgeons (ACS) in 1913 and the American College of Physicians (ACP) in 1915. Paul Starr best described the true measure of how doctors dominated health care in America throughout most of its history in his Pulitzer Prize-winning book, *The Social Transformation of American Medicine* (1982)[1]:

"Yet the replacement of a competitive orientation with a corporate consciousness required more than common interests. It required a transfer of power to the group, and this was what began to happen in medicine around 1900 with changes in its social structure. Physicians came increasingly to rely on each other's good will for their access to patients and facilities. Physicians also depended more on their colleagues for defense against malpractice suits, which were increasing in frequency. The courts, in working out the rules of liability for medical practice in the late nineteenth century, had set as the standard of care that of the local community where the physicians practiced. This limited possible expert testimony against physicians to their immediate colleagues. By adopting the "locality rule," the courts prepared the way for granting considerable power to the local medical society, for it became almost impossible for patients to get testimony against a physician who was a member. Medical societies began to make malpractice defense a direct service. Shortly after the turn of the century, doctors in New York, Chicago, and Cleveland organized common defense funds. The Massachusetts Medical Society began handling malpractice suits in 1908. During the next ten years, it supported accused physicians in all but three of the ninety-four cases it received. Only twelve of these ninety-one cases went to trial, all save one resulting in a victory for the doctor. For its first twenty years, the defense fund of the medical society of the state of Washington won every case it fought. Because of their ability to protect their members, medical societies were able to get low insurance rates, while doctors who did not belong could scarcely get any insurance protection. This provided the sort of "selected incentive" that medical societies needed to help them attract members. Professional ostracism carried increasingly serious consequences: denial of hospital privileges, loss of referrals, loss of malpractice insurance, and in extreme cases, loss of a license to practice. The local medical fraternity became the arbiter of a doctor's position and fortune, and he could no longer choose to ignore it. By making the county societies the gate-keeper to membership in any higher professional group, the AMA had recognized and strengthened the position of the local fraternity, as well as bolstering its own organizational underpinnings."

"Those who cannot remember the past are condemned to repeat it."

—George Santayana

Paul Starr's snapshot of health care in America dramatizes several noteworthy facts. For a 220-year period (1788–2008), medical care has been primarily a capitalistic, consumer-product, much like a loaf of bread, a car, or a house (one purchased as one could afford), and the first 175 years of health care were devoid of significant federal or state governmental involvement. That raw power doctors were able to wield through their newly formed Organized Medicine at the turn of the twentieth century was to last for another half century, but all good things must eventually come to an end. The combination of post WWII and the GI Bill exploded in our midst, and America has never been the same. A health care time line provides some perspective to the history of health care in America (See Appendix A).

Scientific advancements created the previously spoken of change within the medical profession. The era of modern medicine began bringing countless changes to the medical profession, with one being the rapid introduction of a wide range of medical specialization. Family doctors, heretofore the backbone of the profession and the principal source of leadership within the AMA, began their speedy slide into obscurity as numerous specialty organizations began to fragment the solidarity of control held by the original troika (AMA, ACS, ACP). This transfer of professional influence was lamented in the Journal of the AMA (JAMA) as late as the mid '60s.

Organized Medicine, by its very nature of representing the medical profession must be considered as one of the three major components of our health care system, but Organized Medicine should be considered from a proper perspective. People assume, erroneously, that Organized Medicine in general—and AMA, through its tri-level organization of national, state, and local entities—plays a significant part in the regulation of medical practice and patient care. Nothing would be further from the truth.

AMA has gone from Starr's depiction as king of its realm one hundred years ago to a paper tiger today. AMA is in reality the principal lobbyist for Organized Medicine and something akin to the president's press secretary. AMA has zero regulatory power over its members due to the simple fact that should any attempt be made to peer review a member at any of its three levels that attempt would be met with, "I just resigned my AMA membership." End of story. AMA, still Organized Medicine's chief spokesperson with Congress, state legislatures, and the media, is actually more like an aged theatrical star who is most honored for past performances. Doubters may dispute this assessment by providing clear evidence of an active and effective form of practitioner regulation within AMA or any other components of Organized Medicine. None will be found, thus the *paper tiger* pejorative will stand.

The medical profession not only fails society by making no significant contribution in attempting to self-regulate their members, but their contribution to efforts by others to address health care problems is usually cloaked in self-interest. Dr. John Clough[2], recently retired editor in chief of the *Cleveland Clinic Journal of Medicine*, wrote in 1997:

"In the past, the state and county medical societies played a reactionary role in virtually every political debate affecting health care, and to some extent they continue on this path. They have acquired the reputation of opposing whatever the current reform proposal was, while rarely offering a reasonable alternative (or even directly addressing problems everyone inside and outside the health care system knew existed). The societies protected the interests of physicians but were often blind to the needs of society and even to the needs of the patients they served. They were almost never seen as part of the solution, and gradually they came to be viewed as part of the problem. Long adherence to this reactionary approach has so damaged the credibility of the profession that the Clinton administration eschewed physician input when it set out to develop its health care reform plan, one of many mistakes that led to the ultimate failure of that plan."

To understand our current health care system and its many problems, one must begin with Organized Medicine, but viewed with an accurate perspective of exactly how their medical organizations have contributed to those problems and how little those same organizations have contributed to making that system better. Those who view this assessment of Organized Medicine as being too harsh should relax. There is more than enough blame to go around.

States

Private practice of medicine is the least regulated economic activity in America

Health care is assumed to be regulated by fifty states and the federal government, *but* state legislatures are responsible for the regulation of private medical practice and hospital medical staffs. Somehow this obligation to society for the regulation of the practice of medicine failed to be recognized by those fifty state legislatures. This state governmental lapse follows a consistent bureaucratic pattern of legislative ineptitude.

Each state will now have several agencies having separate health care responsibilities and the collaborative intent to effectively regulate health care in their state. That collaborative intent is where the best of intentions becomes a fool's paradise.

State medical examining boards are the state regulatory agencies with the longest history of existence and the strongest record(s) of inefficiency. Never have so many done so little for those they seek to serve. State medical examining boards and medical schools were long considered by the leaders of the medical profession to be their tools for identifying and excluding unqualified aspirants to their profession. Neither have ever been able, each for reasons of its own, to fulfill this necessary task. That is failure number one. Failure number two is Organized Medicine and state legislatures have never united to create a system to properly identify and expel unqualified practitioners, regardless of the constant evidence throughout the nation that unqualified medical practitioners are a plague on society.

The gravity of failure number two goes to the heart of why the quality of health care in America continues to suffer enormous needless patient harm with no evidence of beneficial change and also goes to the heart of the message of this book.

Patient safety can only be adequately improved by first recognizing all of the components of the health care system and where improved regulation must take place.

Other state agencies, with varying titles, will have more recently been legislatively created to manage Medicare, Medicaid, hospitals, other health care facilities and the like. Every state possesses an enormous system of multiple agency health care regulatory effort with little evidence of a desired result. So what went wrong?

States are the stepchild of our national health care system and to make matters worst, there are fifty stepchildren. States had the duty to regulate the private practice of medicine and therefore the majority aspect of all health care in America long before the massive encroachment by the federal government via Medicare and Medicaid in 1965, and most, if not all, were doing nothing. Every state, each in their own way, have been colossal failures in the regulation of health care, and by so doing nothing, state legislatures created the flawed foundation for Organized Medicine and federal and state governments to build our current health care system upon.

The proper way to validate the premise of this accusation was presented in the Introduction. Invite any state to diagram the mechanism created by the collaborative efforts of their various health care agencies and explain precisely how that mechanism was intended to function. People are frantically seeking ways to improve patient care while never demanding to be shown exactly what regulatory system has been created by their state legislature, when it was created, and how it functions. A recent Air France airline tragedy over the South Atlantic has created a frantic search for the airplane's black boxes. State legislatures should be forced to find and examine their "black boxes" containing their mechanism for the regulation of the practice of medicine, hospital medical staffs, and the ever-expanding number of surgery centers. That fifty-state effort would be the first giant step toward vastly improved medical regulation from those who are responsible for such regulation to their entire state population.

Patient safety activists across America should take a lesson from Mothers Against Drunk Drivers (MADD) and unite under one big tent, demanding that every state "find their black box" containing the regulatory mechanism for the private practice of medicine, hospital medical staffs and surgery centers. The urgent need for the search for each state's medical regulatory black box will be more clearly presented in the chapter "How To Fix It."

State legislatures are the most culpable component of our entire health care system regarding the failure to properly regulate patient care. However, there continues to be enough blame to go around.

Federal

Federal involvement in health care is long standing through Department of Defense (DoD) Veterans Administration (VA), Public Health (PH) and such, but that involvement was a relatively small portion of the health care whole until 1965. The fat man made a big splash when he jumped into the health care pool with the two Ms. Euphemistically speaking, Medicare and Medicaid were the first act of medical cloning. Where before 1965, the federal government consumed a small piece of the health care financial pie, after 1965 their piece suddenly became much larger and has continually grown. Initially, federally controlled health care was the *mini-me* compared to what might be called *regular* health care, but federally created programs all too often exhibit cancer-like tendencies and grow by consuming anything they share space with.

Now, federally controlled health care consumes over half of the health care pie, with no end in sight. This is the previously mentioned outside force. This ravenous consumption of the health care financial pie has tragically distorted every attempt to better understand our health care system, its problems, and fundamentally sound ways to react to and correct those problems.

Newsflash—health care is *not* just cost and access. Nor is it cost and access and information technology. Both of those aspects are exceedingly important, but neither singularly nor in combination are they the very heart of health care. Health care is now and has always been doctors (humans) treating patients (other humans) and everyone hopefully seeking to create a system as problem free as possible. We have yet to begin the seeking part.

Federal health care has gone from DoD, VA, PH to NAS, IOM, HHS, CMS, AHRQ, PSRO, PRO, QIO and continues into acronym heaven. With all of this concentrated effort, why don't *things* get better in health care? Because no one can truly say *things* are getting better! The federal government's ravenous consumption of the health care fiscal pie continues, while their attempts to control health care costs are met with failure. Defensive medicine is one of the major reasons (if not *the* major reason) for the constant increase in health care cost and is described as doctors providing unnecessary treatment in an attempt to avoid malpractice. Therefore, one of the vexing quandaries of health care is that the federal government is contributing most of the effort to reduce health care cost, while defensive medicine is a major contributor to that problem, and the states have the direct responsibility to regulate and control the practice of medicine provided by most of the doctors in the nation. Did I loose anyone in all of that?

The first diagram depicts the three major health care components having over-lapping health care responsibilities. What can too easily be lost in viewing this diagram is that while the three major components, Organized Medicine, states, and federal, do have over-lapping, and at times, conflicting health care responsibilities, they also have different responsibilities.

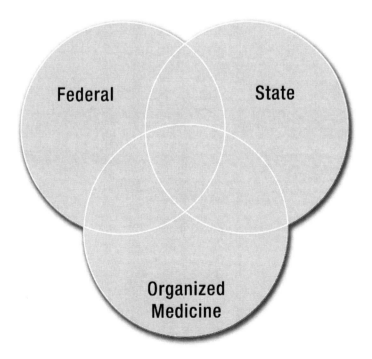

The second diagram shows a triangle has been superimposed where the three circles overlap, because somewhere within that Bermuda triangle, one can find most of the basic elements of the organizational structure of health care in America. Within that black hole of regulatory madness lie the results of over four decades of the three major components of our health care system simultaneously making contributions, while each one was seemingly speaking in different languages.

To begin to make health care order out of health care chaos, one must first be able to clearly identify the health care organizational structure contained within that triangle. Unfortunately, even the need for such rational understanding is yet to be recognized by those participating in the massive effort to "change health care."

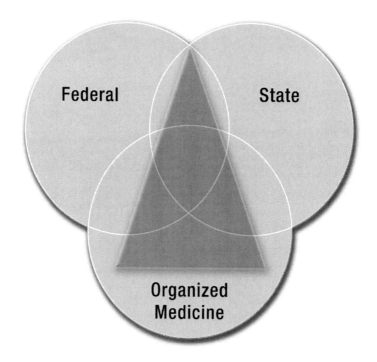

What are the most important elements missing in the administration of our health care system?

Clearly defined:

- *Points of authority*

- *Points of responsibility*

- *Points of accountability*

The development of our health care system satisfies all of the requirements of the Darwin Theory of Evolution: that system has developed via serendipity with no direct input from a source of higher intellect.

The above play on words is not intended to be humorous. Our health care system, one sixth of our entire economy, and a system that will directly impact every person in America, has been allowed to develop like a weed patch with no master plan. People wonder why our health care system is in such a horrible mess while giving little thought as to where we are now and how we got here.

Medical advancements in science and technology have gone *zoom*, and in so doing, obscured the abysmal lack of organizational administration I describe as "Med-Albania" (Albania being the most backward country bordering Western civilization).

However, there are still three lesser components to be included and still more blame to go around.

Minor Components

Minor does not imply lack of significance. Fully understanding our current health care system, its problems and pathways for beneficial change, is impossible without an equal understanding of each minor component. Awareness of grave problems in our health care system is long standing. Perhaps the delay in responsibly dealing with those problems is due, in part, to a failure to recognize all of that system's components that contribute to those problems. These minor, for want of a better term, components make far more than minor contributions to a deeply flawed social system, and many of those contributions are questionable, if not harmful and largely ignored.

Joint Commission

Joint Commission on Accreditation of Healthcare Organizations (JCAHO) was created in 1951, by Organized Medicine initially as the Joint Commission on the Accreditation of Hospitals (JCAH). The significance of that *O* will be described later.

Congress transformed the JC into a quasi-governmental agency with unbelievable financial power over most hospitals and zero congressional oversight with the passage of Medicare and Medicaid in 1965.

No one in or out of Congress seemed to know then, or have recognized since, the enormity of that willful transfer of power granted to an organization dominated by the medical profession.

No complete understanding of our health care system and its immense problems is possible without a complete understanding of the JC role since 1965. Americans with any awareness of current national and international affairs will have an overwhelmingly negative attitude regarding the United Nations. They would have an equally negative attitude toward the JC if all of the truth were made public.

Most of the recent $700 billion bailout of the financial housing market was due to congressional mismanagement. Much of our current health care problems are due to an equal degree of congressional mismanagement, and much of that can be directly related to the JC past record of willful negligence. JC is, first and foremost, an internal arm of Organized Medicine, and Dr. John Clough's previously quoted assessment of where the medical profession's most abiding concern lies offers little encouragement where the public is concerned. The heart of the medical error problem throughout our nation can be laid at the JC doorstep. JC certification of most hospitals and their medical staffs has resulted in absolutely no improvement where the regulation of medical errors is concerned. Later, evidence will be provided to demonstrate how JC is surreptitiously further undermining medical peer review.

Organized Medicine can show no evidence of being the friend of recipients of questionable patient care, and JC is, and has always been, an arm of Organized Medicine. Yet there remains enough blame to go around.

Cottage Industry

No person can name every governmental, non-governmental, public, private, think-tank, foundation, school of public health, other university health care research, etc. that has been creating countless studies on every aspect of health care. Thousands of highly educated and highly dedicated individuals have made making health care better their pursuit in life, and still, patient safety and medical error concerns remain basically unchanged at your local hospital medical staff level. Yet no one seems to ever, publicly at least, wonder why. There have to be understandable reasons why all of this past and current effort has not culminated in a far better quality of health care. One major reason is that no one currently involved in such efforts can describe in detail the organizational structure of that enormous, vital social system they are striving to improve.

Health care has its own cottage industry similar to the current cabal of pundits and polltakers who have turned our election process into a Frankenstein monster. Too many people are making far more money than they ever anticipated, and therefore both of these cottage industries continue to grow and the federal government is the principle source of growth in the health care cottage industry. That would be reassuring news but for the fact that most of that recent governmentally inspired scholarship results in meaningless babble.

Institute of Medicine (IOM) *Crossing the Quality Chasm* series of books offers a snapshot view of the health care cottage industry. A thorough review must include the list of committee members, their respective organizations, the study staff, reviewers, and the list of references, authors, and affiliations. Next, one should begin to note the number of organizations with the word *quality* in their title.

Example: The National Forum for Health Care Quality Measurement and Reporting (National Quality Forum or NQF) became operational in 2000, as a public-private partnership at the behest of the President's Advisory Commission on Consumer Protection and Quality in the Healthcare Industry. "NQF mission is to improve American healthcare through endorsement of consensus-based national standards for measurement and public reporting of healthcare performance data that provide meaningful information about whether care is safe, timely, beneficial, patient-centered, equitable and efficient." They do not do windows or take out the garbage.

Note: IOM launched a concerted, ongoing effort focused on assessing and improving the nation's quality of care in 1996. NQF began its quest for measurement of quality health care in 2000. To repeat, still patient safety and medical error concerns remain basically unchanged at your local hospital medical staff level. Why?

Opposing hypotheses will clash during the later discussion of the health care cottage industry, and the public needs to fully understand the importance of that difference in theoretical methodology offered in the next chapter (What Went Wrong?).

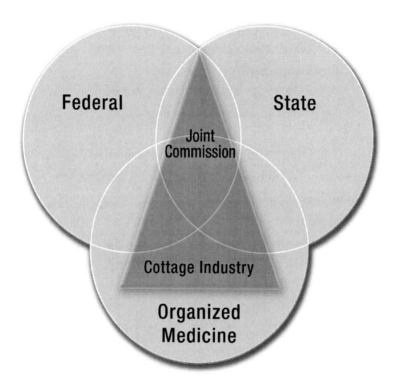

Current health care cottage industry research methodology supports mandated medical standards of care created by "experts on Mount Olympus" to be promulgated down to the doctor-patient inter-face at the local level. Read the IOM current series of *Crossing the Quality Chasm* books and discover the science fiction of federally created medical standards of care.

Specific individual-practitioner medical standards of care created at the local doctor-patient interface will also be presented and supported by past, little recognized, positive steps in greatly increased patient safety as a stark contrast and is presented in the chapter "What Went Right." As an experienced practitioner, I find the mass of health care cottage industry recommendations and conclusions for quality improvements involving patient care to be immensely harmful and misguided. Let the debate begin.

Still one "minor" component remains to be considered.

800,000 Doctors

Health care begins with doctors, yet few health care experts seem to include that indispensable element in their recipe for health care change. There is a lot of anger within our medical profession, and some of it is even justified. Doctors, being all too human, display the typical characteristic of turning a blind eye to their shortcomings by viewing their problem as being somebody else's fault!

Our health care system has two developmental flaws;

- *Aforementioned Darwin form of development.*

- *Capitalistic form of economic, consumer product system.*

I defy anyone to answer, unequivocally, that aged-old question, "Is health care a right or a privilege?" Many can answer that question philosophically one way or the other, but our national heritage of being founded on a capitalistic economic system denies the luxury of one choice over the other. Demands for future change from our present model to a radically different form of health care cannot erase the past history or current reality. In spite of Michael Moore's absurd movie *Sicko* and the cries for universal health care, there is *no* magic wand.

Speaking from experience, most doctors enter the profession with aspirations to make a better than average living, raise a family, chase the American dream, and be a benefit to society at the same time. Experts talk about radically changing health care as though doctors were not a factor to be considered. Universal health care says what to the vast majority of our current medical practitioners? Are doctors to be conscripted into a new, socialized system of health care as an afterthought?

Federal

State

Joint
Commission

800,000

Cottage Industry

Organized
Medicine

Doctors are the greatest source of fault in creating most of the health care problems we face today, but for a little recognized reason. Individually and collectively, doctors have failed to contribute to all efforts to create a more modern health care system. Dr. Clough clearly pointed out how doctors have consistently been a major obstacle to beneficial health care change. Doctors were passively given full authority over one of the most important social systems in our nation for almost two hundred years, and they turned their profession into a good-old-boy network by putting self-interest before the society they had sworn to serve.

Our medical profession can offer zero evidence of any credible effort toward self-regulation of its members. When doctors were most in control they chose to circle the wagons and leave harmed patients at the mercy of attorneys, courts, and lay juries. Still, there can be no health care system without doctors.

Organizational Infrastructure

All of the elements of the organizational infrastructure of health care can be found in this working model. The problem to face is, will anyone seek to clearly define our health care system's organizational infrastructure? The need for such an understanding has, to date, apparently been ignored.

Evolution of health care in America truly does satisfy Darwin's theory of serendipity's part in the creation of great things. Our current health care system was developed by three major sources, each imbued with self-interest.

Organized Medicine, originally the sole owner, is infuriated with the new, uninvited partners.

States have acted like children given a toy to play with that is far beyond their comprehension. State's rights, long ago, gave each state the right and the responsibility to regulate economic activity within their borders as they saw fit.

The private practice of medicine is the least regulated economic activity.

Congress has usurped a position of majority ownership, in spite of having negligible knowledge and understanding of the subject.

To quote Dr. David Gratzer, in his 2006 book *The Cure,* "The problem and the predicament of American health care can be stated in a single, paradoxical sentence: Everyone agrees that it's the best in the world, but nobody really likes it."

While there is much truth in Dr. Gratzer's statement, unfortunately he does not go on to tell his readers why there is so much truth in that statement. I will.

Meaningful health care change can only be accomplished by placing the three missing points of *authority, responsibility,* and *accountability* in their proper place(s).

Defense Department can provide a complete organizational chart from the Secretary of Defense down to the newest recruits in each of the military services, including the above three points. Is it too much to ask that Organized Medicine, each state legislature, and Congress do the same regarding health care?

Role Model

Flexner report: One hundred years ago, the Carnegie Foundation commissioned Abraham Flexner, a man with no medical education, to do a two-year study of medical education in America and Canada and report his findings and recommendations.

Flexner found:

- More than 150 schools, enrolling some 25,000 students.

- Nearly half of the world's medical students were crowded into American schools.

- A dozen schools offered quality instruction.

- Approximately twenty other schools stood out above the rest.

His two-part report described the historical evolution of medical education and offered his recommendation for the minimum requirements of medical education and then included his study of all of the schools with suggestions for which ones appeared to be worth supporting.

Flexner, very soon after, repeated a similar study of medical education in most of the countries of Western Europe. Fifty years later, and just prior to his death, he was honored as having made the greatest single contribution to the advancement of medical education here and in Europe.

What must be learned from Abraham Flexner as a role model for those who will participate in the process of changing health care in America today?

First, Flexner began his study by describing the historical evolution of the subject he was to recommend changes for, medical education.

Second, all of the over one hundred unworthy medical schools—but one—had been closed twenty years after his report in 1910.

Lesson: Meaningful change does not occur overnight except in the minds of politicians who love to promise the impossible.

Iconoclast: Abraham Flexner and A Life in Learning by Thomas Neville Bonner for those who would seek a better understanding of this remarkable man.

Summary

Change health care now! A stampede of people, one can assume having the best of intentions, are racing to change a huge, vital, social system none of them can describe in detail, and no one is suggesting caution.

Change is not always for the better!

Our health care system is horribly flawed and far less than it could be or should be, but mindless change has little chance of making it better.

Since there is more than enough blame to go around to all of the participants in the system, let's next seek to find what went wrong, where, and why, while keeping Flexner's example of detail understanding prior to action in mind.

WHAT WENT WRONG?

Major Components

Health care as we know it today began with the Era of Modern Medicine following the end of WWII and fueled by the GI Bill and a horde of returning veterans now mature enough to seek education and careers far beyond pre-WWII imaginations. America began a rapid transformation in every segment of society, and health care was one of the flash points.

In 1950, Organized Medicine, primarily through the AMA, was the only one of the six current components of health care that could invoke significant input into the organizational structure of that system. Doctors were just doctors in those days, federal and state governments were relatively silent in the administration of health care, and the JC and CI were yet to see the light of day.

In the next sixty-odd years, health care would become a giant, poorly organized, highly mismanaged, major segment of how America represents itself today. Our current health care system gives the impression that the inmates have taken over the asylum. No aspect of health care truly functions as it should, and no one appears to be asking, "How did this happen?"

Acknowledging there is enough blame to go around, let's review each component's contribution to this present debacle.

Organized Medicine

Review the JAMA from 1949–2003, as I did, and you will see the two faces of Organized Medicine, each in stark contrast to the other.

Initially, the AMA Leadership said all of the right things as best illustrated by this quote:

> *JAMA, October 1958:* "What marks a profession? It is obligated to assure the public of the competence of its member and the quality of their work. It is obligated to assume the responsibility of disciplining those who do not measure up to the accepted ethical practices of the profession. Only physicians can judge the competence of their colleagues and can prohibit the kinds of conduct harmful to patients and the profession."

That dramatic soliloquy is precisely what the word profession implies and what every patient has always assumed what they would receive. That quote, while speaking volumes, is only one of many such quotes issued by the AMA in the early years of the new Era of Modern Medicine. Unfortunately for both sides of the medical equation, the AMA's eloquent rhetoric became hollow promises.

AMA even went so far as to create a Grievance Committee system in the late 1940s, which was vigorously pursued by their national leadership, but it rapidly became unworkable at the local level where it was to function. It vanished from the JAMA pages by 1965. In truth, the Grievance Committees' primary purpose was to arbitrate fee disputes between doctors and patients. The fact is their good intentions of fulfilling their self-professed "obligation to assume …," etc. were "sound and fury, signifying nothing."[3]

Organized Medicine has never created, nor ever attempted to create, a functional system whereby doctors, the best judge(s) of other doctors, might self-regulate the practice of medicine within their own profession and without attorneys, courts, and juries.

Reality and time eroded even their original "good intentions" of October 1958, and the more recent statements reveal a far different side of Organized Medicine. The first quote is from an AMA brochure titled "Will Your Doctor Be There?" It was published in support of seeking federal medical malpractice tort reform, which, thus far, has fortunately never been enacted.

The primary cause of America's medical liability crisis is overzealous, personal injury attorneys who put their pocketbooks before patients.

An AMA past president and possessor of both MD and JD degrees made the following three quotes at different times.

"Doctors, under the law, if you're treating a patient and you fall below a standard of care SET BY THE LAW and those standards are determined by experts, and that directly causes damage to a patient, that's medical malpractice." (He is defining medical malpractice on a Continuing Medical Education video for doctors.)

"We do know the medical liability system does not measure negligence."

"The law requires a minimally acceptable level of care, thus my analogy to the 'low hurdle.'"

So, medical malpractice is treatment beneath a standard of care set by the law, and that litigation system does not measure negligence, and the legally acceptable medical standard of care is set at the lowest possible hurdle. (His words, not mine.) Tie those revelations with the fact that there is *no* medical malpractice without expert witness testimony, and every expert witness for a patient is vilified and stigmatized in the community in which they practice. I speak from experience. Is it any wonder that doctors seem to almost always win medical malpractice trials?

There is little evidence that any of these quotes, individually, created a measurable response. Collectively, they should portray an ominous image to that constantly growing number of medically harmed patients. Recipients of questionable medical care must ask themselves how, when, and where did an "overzealous personal injury attorney" cause my medical problem?

The other three quotes made by that dual degree AMA past president presents the ingredients for a most insightful presentation of the underlying failures found within the medical malpractice litigation system. Please follow closely as I connect the dots and create a vivid picture of elements known and unknown regarding questionable patient care.

Questionable patient care classifies the target subject far better than more common labels, i.e. medical malpractice, negligent care, and other guilt-before-judgment terms. Questionable patient care clearly supports the understanding that not all patient care problems predicate doctor error, and supports the further understanding that medical care is not a perfect science and that less-than-desirable outcomes may be attributed to non-practitioner causes.

A medical standard of care is inherent in every form of medical care and is the basis upon which all findings of questionable patient care must be based by all three systems of review, state medical examining boards, malpractice litigation, and medical peer review. Also, the term *medical standard of care,* as evident from the above quotes, frequently requires clarifying additions, i.e. "set by the law," "legally acceptable," etc.

Patients, on the other hand, assume they will receive treatment meeting a *current* and *acceptable* standard of care. The wide variation between a current and acceptable medical standard of care and a legally acceptable standard of care set at the lowest possible hurdle creates the following relationship.

STANDARD of CARE

Patient assumes	Current and Acceptable

ZONE of DIFFERENCE

Legally acceptable	Lowest possible hurdle

*Substandard—Negligence—Malpractice

A far better understanding of questionable patient care can be gained by identifying the elements of patient care missing from the above diagram.

*Saran wrap rule: The equivalent of a layer of Saran wrap separates legally acceptable medical standard of care set at the lowest possible hurdle from negligent or malpractice care.

More importantly, four classes of doctors based upon their personal patient care capability can be identified within that zone of difference.

STANDARD of CARE

Patient assumes	Current and Acceptable

1. Doctors unqualified to retain a medical license.

2. Doctors with limited capabilities due to age, etc., who should be limited in their scope of practice.

3. Doctors utilizing out-dated treatment techniques.

4. Good doctors who have made a human error but demonstrate a current and acceptable patient care track record.

Legally acceptable	Lowest possible hurdle

Substandard—Negligence—Malpractice

Doctors detest the medical malpractice litigation system primarily because it can't distinguish between those four classes of doctors, and therefore, the good doctors get tarnished with the less capable doctors. That system of medical malpractice litigation will never be able to distinguish between the wide variance in doctor qualifications, so that leaves us with this question:

What went wrong within Organized Medicine?

The same thing that goes wrong in too many marriages, businesses, and many other forms of human endeavor. Doctors, like all the rest of us, are all too human. Doctors spend so many years high on a pedestal that they are unable to handle well just being another clog in the system.

Doctors owe society ethical behavior and self-regulation and all of the other attributes of a profession. The JAMA October 1958 quote shows their previous desire to provide those things. But all of us humans seem to put self-interest first when push comes to shove.

Questionable patient care happens. Doctors are only human, and questionable patient care will always continue to be a fact of medical life. There are now, and have always been, only three systems with the potential to review questionable patient care. State medical examining boards have never been and can never be an acceptable system for that purpose. That leaves only two viable systems with the potential to review questionable patient care: malpractice litigation and medical peer review.

That is what went wrong within Organized Medicine.

Doctors long ago chose medical malpractice litigation (attorneys, courts, and juries) as the principle system for the review of questionable patient care. They left society with sue or forget it and continue, in every way, to speak as though that is the only system of patient care review available to them. A review of Paul Starr's stark portrayal of the gangster-like hold Organized Medicine held on the practice of medicine and all of health care in the early 1900s illustrates how medical malpractice litigation was then, and continues to be, the principle tool used by that profession in their scheme of self-regulation.

Organized Medicine made the wrong choice.

Medical peer review is the only system of the three available where doctors are in control. Properly used medical peer review allows doctors to judge other doctors without attorneys, courts, and juries. I know, because over thirty years ago, I was a member of a hospital medical peer review committee that removed all of the hospital privileges from a surgeon with twenty-five years experience because he used out-dated forms of patient care and refused to change.

The moment an attorney becomes involved as a patient's agent seeking review of questionable patient care, the medical profession looses all control of the process. The major problem within our medical profession is, and has always been, the use of civil courts as the principle tool for the review of questionable patient care.

The only solution to that problem will be found when a vast majority of all questionable patient care review will take place within medical peer review and without attorneys, courts and juries. Such a system is far more attainable than imagined and will be presented later.

States

Fifty states play an important part in contributing to the organizational structure of our health care system, and all have played their part poorly.

State medical examining boards were the only tool of state medical regulation of health care prior to 1950. Now there's a different story. South Carolina is reported to have seventy-two state agencies (three regarding health care) employing over 65,000 people and over 250 boards and commissions. That summary represents a lot of people constantly working to make things better. So what went wrong in health care?

Consider these three tragic events that actually occurred at different times in my Upstate South Carolina community.

First Event: A construction worker is accidentally

killed at the work site. OSHA investigators are on the scene within hours.

Second Event: A single-engine airplane crashes on take-off. Both occupants walk away with only slight injuries. FAA investigators are at the site within hours.

Third Event: A twenty-seven-year-old, slender, healthy woman enters the hospital operating room for minor knee surgery under local anesthesia. She is injected once in the upper thigh area on the front and once in the buttocks. Within minutes, she suffers a catastrophic system collapse, and within a few additional minutes, *she is clinically dead!*

No investigators from any regulatory agency ever appeared at the site of that tragedy. Her widowed husband was forced to sue the doctors in order to find out what happened. *On the third anniversary of her death, a lay jury returned a verdict of no negligence.* The doctors had won another court case.

Hospitals are the only site in America where an accidental death can occur and receive no regulatory, in-depth investigation. The practice of medicine is the least regulated economic activity. Both failures are the responsibility of state legislatures.

States had (and still have) far more regulatory power to create an organizational structure for the regulation of health care than any other health care component, and each one has failed to do so. The only way to fully understand the depth of those failures is to force each state to document each past, step-by-step process taken in the creation of their respective current system of health care regulation.

South Carolina has created a system of health care administration composed primarily of three departments:

- Department of Health and Human Services (DHHS)

- Department of Health and Environmental Control (DHEC)

- State Medical Examining Board (SMEB)

Everyone presumes those three agencies' combined efforts have created a health care regulatory system. That system permitted that twenty-seven-year-old wife and mother to tragically die an accidental death in a hospital and have her death be totally ignored by the very system that was supposedly created to protect her. Worse still, that tragedy occurred approximately eight years ago, and *nothing* involving regulatory response to such tragedies has changed! State legislatures make Congress look like rocket scientists.

People can drown in the volume of patient safety literature at the same time that no real progress is evident in the reality of day-to-day patient safety where it matters most. States are the most important sites for making the greatest and most rapid improvement in patient safety, and none of the health care quality experts are even talking about directing their focus in that direction.

Abraham Flexner gave us the best clue on how to understand what went wrong in every state regarding health care. *First, he began his study by describing the historical evolution of the subject he was to recommend changes for—medical education.* Such a study of any state's health care organizational structure will demonstrate that each state legislature has, over time, created a multi-agency, mechanical system with no mind, no heart, and no soul. Each state has a system created for humans by regulating the actions of other humans that is devoid of any human characteristics.

There is one other major aspect that must be considered in how and why the states, individually and collectively, have so miserably failed in their responsibility to provide health care regulation. While states were finally beginning to realize they must take part in regulating health care in the '50s and '60s, Congress was simultaneously awakening to their opportunity to participate in health care regulation, and thus began *The Blurring of the Lines of Regulatory Power between Congress and States.*

There is total confusion and chaos in health care regulation because the critical points of *authority, responsibility,* and *accountability* cannot be clearly identified between the major players. Who's on first?

Federal

Blurring of the lines of authority, responsibility, and accountability between federal and state governments is one of the major harmful contributions to health care by the federal government. Congress creates bureaucracies and regulatory agencies the way too many people raise their children—with no parental supervision.

The absence of clear lines of authority between federal and state agencies, and the scarcity of thorough over-sight and accountability are critical factors in the current health care chaos. Two seldom discussed examples of how Congress' best intentions can so easily and rapidly become more a burden than an asset.

PSRO–PRO–QIO: When Congress created Medicare/Medicaid in 1965, it also created multiple opportunities for abuse. Congress demands accountability (of others far more than of itself), and therefore it created the system of Professional Standards Review Organizations (PSRO) in 1972 (seven years later). Medicare PSRO is *not* the same system of medical peer review that should be inherent within the medical profession, but far too many people confuse the two.

To add to the confusion, Congress dismantled the PSRO system and created the Peer Review Organization (PRO) in 1982. Now PRO has been joined or replaced by the

Quality Improvement Organization (QIO) system. Readers interested in the governmental jungle of acronyms can pursue that on their own.

What's important and largely unknown about all the congressional name changing? There are fifty-three QIO organizations spread across the nation, and they have established the American Health Quality Association (AHQA), as a private organization to represent their members. Two quotes by AHQA Executive Vice President David Schulke will tell you far more than Congress seems to know or consider important.

American Medical News, September 3, 2001: "PROs are focused on preventing quality problems from recurring, rather than figuring out who is responsible for what failings and punishing people."

American Medical News, July 8, 2002: "About 90% of complaints to the PROs deal with billing problems and other non-clinical issues."

So Congress created a system of Medicare medical peer review over thirty years ago with literature filled with phrases such as "meets professionally recognized standards of care," and the words "standards" and "quality," but did *not* intend to figure out who is responsible for what failing, and 90 percent of the complaints they deal with are billing problems and other non-clinical issues.

Perhaps rather than asking, "What went wrong?" The question should be, "Did anything go right?"

National Practitioner Data Bank (NPDB): NPDB was established in 1986 and began collecting and disseminating information in 1990. It's intent was to improve the quality of health care by encouraging state licensing boards, hospitals and other health care entities, and professional societies to identify and discipline those who engage in unprofessional behavior; and to restrict the ability of incompetent physicians, dentists, and other health care practitioners to move from state to state without disclosure or discovery of previous medical malpractice payment and adverse action history.

There should come a time when the "best of intentions" are over-whelmed by the facts of the track record. First, in spite of three name changes, the Medicare review system is *not* concerned with who might be causing problems and are primarily focused upon "billing problems and other non-clinical issues," and second, the newspapers and magazines continue to write stories of doctors who have left a trail of broken bodies in multiple states in spite of almost twenty years existence with the NPDB.

The first page of my first book, *First, Do No Harm, The Cure for Medical Malpractice,* describes how an orthopedic surgeon, lacking the titanium rod needed to stabilize a patient's spine, inserted a screwdriver instead. The screwdriver broke in two days and was removed. After three more surgeries the patient was left a bedridden, incontinent paraplegic and soon died. That travesty occurred in Hilo, Hawaii, after that surgeon had been run out of Oklahoma and Texas for drug addiction and incompetence. The malpractice trial was two years later, but there was no mention of the NPDB, which had been in operation for over ten years.

When will we ever learn that all congressmen and state legislators know very little about most things? Many may be very knowledgeable about certain subjects, but the reality is, they don't know what they don't know about most of the issues they not only vote on, but speak freely about. Congressmen and state legislators should have to take and pass an "Are You Smarter Than a 5th Grader" exam prior to voting on key legislation. Yet Congress, with the advice of others, had created the NPDB to identify doctors such as this Hilo, Hawaii, nutcase.

There are three problems identified here: the NPDB is still doing its thing, there is no evidence "its thing" has been even partially beneficial, and Congress ignores that agency's failure to provide the anticipated protection, and why that two decade-old agency failure occurred. Many vague reasons have long been given for the inefficiency of the NPDB, but the resultant lack of real value to the unsuspecting public is tolerated year after year. Congress at its best.

Make a list of key social issues, i.e., health care, immigration, social security, etc. Most, if not all, are in dire straits, primarily due to congressional mismanagement. Now "they" want to "fix" your health care system, and most people seem comfortable with that prospect. Now, there is a stampede for those same people to "work their magic" on our health care system.

A full appreciation of how federal intervention into health care beginning in 1965, needed or not, has created as much confusion as benefit requires an understanding of the two themes of this segment:

- Blurring of the lines of responsibility.

- Absence of clearly defined points of *authority*, *responsibility* and *accountability*.

The story gets no better when the minor components are considered.

Minor Components

Joint Commission

Nothing went wrong in health care from the JC perspective. Congress created the JC we know today, and Congress has left the JC "master of their domain." That is until last fall. There is a new game in town, and the JC now has competition. DNV Healthcare was "deemed" by Congress to also certify hospitals for Medicare. DNV will be discussed more fully later, because they have had too little time to develop a recognizable track record thus far.

Everything went wrong in health care from a patient safety perspective. Doubters *must* read the literature.

Never events—a new term in the patient safety lexicon, which describes preventable and should-never-happen patient care events. That twenty-seven-year-old wife and mother who anticipated minor knee surgery under local anesthesia and ended up dead was certainly a never event. There is no mention of the JC in connection with that or any other similar *event*.

Joint Commission was anointed the nation's royal certifier of 80 percent of all hospitals over four decades ago, and the results are clearly evident but strangely ignored. Never events continue to occur at an alarming and consistent rate, while hospitals and medical staffs of widely varying degrees of competence continue to be certified. There is a reason for that medical carnage in the midst of volumes of patient safety rhetoric, but one must connect the dots to disclose that reason.

Organized medicine created the JC in 1951, but Congress made them a far greater health care power than anyone could have ever imagined. They magnanimously gave the JC certifying power over the Medicare dollar and conveyed that power under a cockamamie, congressional, contractual basis with little oversight. (*How* little will be provided later.)

In 1987, JCAH became JCAHO when H (hospitals) became HO (health care organizations). The JC also announced their initiation of "The Agenda for Change."

Within one year their agenda for change became their idealistic rhetoric.

Wall Street Journal, October 12, 1988: "Small Comfort: Prized by Hospitals, Accreditation Hides Perils Patients Face," by Walt Bogdanich.

One brief segment of that most informative article offers much insight into JC accreditation. Full accreditation was given to New York City's Parson's Hospital after a June 1986 "inspection," and it remained "fully accredited." New York State closed Parson's Hospital in May 1988 after seventy-three patients died between October 1, 1987 and April 18, 1988. The JC removed that hospital's accreditation one week later, and New York State ended its long-standing arrangement with the JC. Yet there was no evidence of congressional interest in what some might consider to be a very important disclosure of possible hospital accreditation ineptness.

Selected quotes from that article are quite illuminating:

"Although accreditation is voluntary, many hospitals couldn't survive without it. Accredited hospitals qualify for Medicare reimbursements, the single greatest source of revenue for hospitals."

"The Joint Commission, based in Chicago, is one of the most powerful and secretive groups in all of health care."

"The Joint Commission allows dangers to health and safety to go uncorrected for weeks, months and even years. Sloppy, irresponsible hospitals have little to fear from the Commission: punishment in recent years has been nearly nonexistent."

"Parson's failed its commission inspection. Yet the JC waited nearly a full year, until May 28, 1987, before reporting its findings in writing to Parson's officials. In a cover letter of the same date, the JC told Parson's Hospital it could, nevertheless, appeal the findings of its 'recent' inspection."

"The JC concedes that it can't always identify new problems in hospitals as quickly as it would like. Amid much fanfare, it has announced an Agenda for Change, whereby it would measure a hospital's actual performance, not just its ability to meet standards."

So, the JC promised significant change and improvement. Fast-forward fourteen years, to another scathing, in-depth article documenting horrendous failings in the JC system of hospital accreditation.

Chicago Tribune, November 10, 2002: "Patients Suffer as Agency Shields Troubled Hospitals," by Michael J. Berens and Bruce Japsen:

"They are bought and paid for by the people they investigate, which is an absolute conflict of interest. It is not a role for hospitals to say we are going to have our own internal auditors. They should be more responsible to us," said Pete Stark of California, who has been in Congress since 1973. He was a senior member of the Ways and Means Committee and has been a Chairman of its health subcommittee.

These two articles are a must-read for those who seek to understand the vast difference between the public persona of the JC and the frightening truth about the true nature of their certifying process.

Additional information will increase a reader's appreciation of the true relationship between Congress, DHHS, and JC, but first one must come to know the DHHS players regarding JC "oversight."

- Department of Health and Human Services (DHHS)

- Office of Inspector General (OIG)

- Office of Evaluation and Inspections (OEI)

- Health Care Financing Administration (HCFA)

- Now Centers for Medicare and Medicaid Services (CMS)

DHHS is charged with JC oversight and instructed their OIG office to initiate a review. OIG assigned their OEI office in Boston, MA, to conduct the JC review beginning in 1997. That review lasted for over one year and culminated with a five-part report entitled "The External Review of Hospital Quality." Excerpts from some of those separate reports will allow the reader to reach their own conclusion regarding JC oversight.

OEI-01–97–00050: A Call for Greater Accountability:
Findings:

The current system of hospital oversight has significant strengths that help protect patients.

JC surveys provide an important vehicle for reducing risk and fostering improvement.

State agency investigations offer a timely, publicly accountable means for responding. But it also has major deficiencies.

JC surveys are unlikely to detect substandard patterns of care or individual practitioners with questionable skills.

State agencies rarely conduct routine, not-for-cause surveys of non-accredited hospitals.

Overall, the hospital review system is moving toward a *collegial* mode of oversight and away from a *regulatory* mode.

JC, the dominant force in external hospital review, is leading this movement.

State agencies are rooted in a more regulatory approach to oversight. But HCFA is looking for them to follow the JC's lead.

The emerging dominance of the *collegial* mode may undermine the existing system of patient protection.

HCFA does little to hold either the JC or the state agencies accountable for their performance overseeing hospitals.

JC objected to the reports conclusion that they (JC) devote minimal attention to complaints.

OEI-01–97–00051: The Role of Accreditation:

JC's reliance on unannounced surveys is limited. From June 1995 through May 1998, it conducted such surveys on about 5% of its accredited hospitals.

Conclusions: Unquestionably, the JC is the central force in the external review of hospital quality. It accredits about 80 percent of the hospitals in the country; and for Medicare purposes, it has a congressionally granted deeming status that is unique among accrediting bodies. Medicare beneficiaries and others who rely upon hospital services have much at stake in how and how well the JC does its job. Our review underscores that the core element of the JC's approach to accreditation is the announced, on-site survey of hospitals—a survey that is heavily oriented toward educational and performance improvement objectives. The other elements of external review—unannounced surveys, responses to complaints, and serious incidents, and standardized performance measures—play relatively minor roles in the JC's accreditation process.

OEI-01–97–00053: Holding the Reviewers Accountable:

Findings: HCFA obtains limited information on the performance of the JC or the states. In both cases, HCFA asks for little in the way of routine performance reports. To assess the JC performance HCFA relies mainly on validation surveys conducted by the state agencies. But for a number of reasons, the value of these surveys has been limited.

HCFA provides limited feedback to the JC and the state agencies on their overall performance. The major vehicle for feedback to the JC is its annual Report to Congress, which is based on the flawed validation surveys and has typically been submitted years late. Public disclosure plays only a minimal role in holding JC and state agencies accountable.

Conclusion: The clear and disturbing conclusion of this report is that both the JC, and state agencies are only minimally accountable to HCFA (now CMS) for their performance in reviewing hospitals.

This is the conclusion of excerpts taken from the DHHS, OIG, OEI review of the JC over ten years ago. There is no evidence that further review of the JC has been conducted by the DHHS apparatus even in light of that second in-depth indictment of the entire JC certification process that appeared in the JC hometown newspaper, the Chicago Tribune in November 2002.

OIG Work Plan Fiscal Year 2008—Oversight of the JC Accreditation Process:

"We will review CMS's (was HCFA) policies and procedures regarding the JC hospital accreditation process (OEI; 00–00–00000; expected issue date: FY

2009; new start)." Unfortunately, that planned follow-up review of the JC accreditation process has been put on hold, even though it has been ten years since the last, highly questionable JC review had taken place. Also a new health care company has recently been approved to compete with JC in the hospital accreditation process for Medicare, DNV Healthcare. More about this company will be provided later, but there is still more about JC.

Earlier, in Chapter 1 (Components of Health Care), I said that evidence would be provided to demonstrate how JC is surreptitiously further undermining medical peer review, the only one of the three systems with the potential to review questionable patient care where doctors are in control of the process and no attorneys, courts, and juries are necessary.

The Medical Staff Handbook: A Guide to Joint Commission Standards, 2nd Edition, 2004: "Purpose of This Book: The Medical Staff Handbook has been developed for hospitals as a guide to *credentialing, privileging,* and *appointing* health care practitioners through the medical staff process."

"The book provides a thorough description of the Medical Staff Chapter of the *Comprehensive Accreditation Manual for Hospitals* (CAMH), which underwent a detailed review and revision resulting in a revised chapter. It also fully describes the standards related to medical staff bylaws, credentialing, privileging, appointment, *competence assessment,* and *performance improvement.*"

So the JC developed a 168 page manual to help hospital medical staffs better assess the *competence* and *performance* of their medical staff members (medical peer review), and presented their new revision of same in the following manner.

FOCUSED PRACTITIONER REVIEW

There are circumstances when focused review of a practitioner's performance and evaluation of such performance by peers (formerly "peer review") are needed to fully assess a practitioner's competence. The organized medical staff must have a process that defines the minimum set of circumstances where focused practitioner review is warranted and when external reviewers are necessary. The goal of this process should not necessarily be disciplinary in nature but primarily to improve practitioner performance.

The focused review process involves monitoring, analyzing, and understanding those special circumstances of practitioners, as defined by the organized medical staff, which requires further evaluation. The organized medical staff is involved in the following:

- Identification of the specific circumstances requiring focused review.

- Identification of the method used to select focused review panels for specific circumstances, including the definition of a peer for the circumstances being reviewed.

- Definition of time frames for focused review activities and adherence to these time frames.

- Evaluation of individuals with clinical privileges whose performance is questioned as a result of measurement and assessment activities.

- Communication to the appropriate parties of the findings, conclusions, recommendations, and actions taken to improve practitioner performance.

- Implementation of changes to improve performance.

The focused review of a practitioner's performance is conducted by his or her peers. The individual whose performance is being reviewed is allowed to participate in the review process as specified by the organized medical staff. Relevant information developed from the focused review process is integrated into PI initiatives and is consistent with hospital preservation of confidentiality and privilege of information.

That is all there is to the JC new methodology for what historically and functionally has always been called medical peer review, and the entire process is given one half of one page out of 168 pages that include "descriptions of standards related to medical staff competence assessment and performance improvement." Presumably, the term *focused* imparts a sense of obligatory need that will finally permeate all hospital medical staffs.

I continue to repeat myself because it is so important that every interested person fully understand. There are now and have always been only three systems with the *potential* to review questionable patient care: state medical examining boards, malpractice litigation, and medical peer review. However, I hold firm to the belief that state medical examining boards have *never* and can *never* provide acceptable questionable patient care review. Hospital medical staffs *are*, by far, the *only* site for efficient questionable patient care review, and the less said about medical malpractice litigation the better.

Assessment in Reality:

- AMA says, "standards of care are set by the law," "the litigation system does not measure negligence," and "the legally acceptable standard of care is set at the lowest possible hurdle."

- JC says, "We are not police."

- DHHS says, "We provide oversight of the JC in order to protect the public."

- States say, "We rely on the JC for hospital medical staff competence."

Conclusion: Regulation and control of the practice of medicine and of hospital medical staffs is non-existent.

Does anyone care?

Federal and state health care agencies, hospital administrations and medical staff leaders, and most health care cottage industry entities speak reverently about the JC and their role in how our health care system currently functions. Therefore, it is difficult to contradict such over-whelming support. JC documented track record, however, should raise concern, if properly scrutinized.

The deciding issue for judging the value of the JC hospital and medical staff certification process should be one's assessment of where we are regarding patient safety and medical errors. If the belief is that discernable progress is clearly evident in regard to those patient care issues, then a favorable assessment of the JC certification process is in order. If, on the other hand, the belief is that regarding patient safety and medical errors, the more things change, the more they remain the same, then one must question the true value of the JC *and* precisely how beneficial their past performance has been to our national health care system as a whole.

I believe the JC has done far more harm than good within our health care system, and much of that harm is due to the broad, but mistaken, belief that they have been a positive asset. No one should reach his or her own conclusion without reading the literature. Nothing provided in this segment is classified secret.

A system of medical peer review that goes into far more detail is offered later in the book as one of the measures that can be taken to rapidly improve the quality of health care and the review of questionable patient care. Perhaps the JC will consider testing the two systems of medical peer review. Since we now have competition in the hospital accreditation process with the arrival of DNV Healthcare, the time should be ideal for testing various methods of questionable patient care review.

Cottage Industry

Mantra: No person can name every governmental, non-governmental, public, private, think-tank, foundation, school of public health, other university health care research, etc. that has been involved in health care research for the last several decades. That incantation remains true, but the composition of the health care cottage industry has changed. Early in health care research, the various public, private, and foundational elements were distinguishable, and there was far less governmental participation. Today, governmental health care research is far greater and includes quasi-governmental organizations created by Congress and then "released" to the public-private sector.

Today's health care cottage industry has far more governmental research participation, and many of the various entities have coalesced into one big, amorphous conglomerate. Current health care research contains input from governmental, public, private, and foundational contributors combined into one and resulting in a consensus of the fundamental elements necessary for establishing quality health care guidelines that can be dispersed throughout the health care system.

A strong sense of collegial agreement has been growing for the past decade that this newly united effort to finally be able to establish greatly improved patient care guidelines is rapidly coming to fruition. A brief summary of several of the more publicized efforts will permit readers to judge for themselves.

The National Forum for Health Care Quality Measurement and Reporting: Commonly known as The National Quality Forum (NQF) and established by Congress in January 1998 for the purpose of promoting the quality, appropriateness, and effectiveness of health care.

NQF process to be used was to arrange for the development and periodic review and updating of:

1. Clinically relevant guidelines that may be used by physicians, educators, and health care practitioners to assist in determining how diseases, disorders, and other health conditions can most effectively and appropriately be prevented, diagnosed, treated, and managed clinically.

2. Standards of quality, performance measures, and medical review criteria through which health

care providers and other appropriate entities may assess or review the provision of health care and assure the quality of such care.

NQF Mission Statement says it will "improve American healthcare through endorsement of consensus-bases national standards for measurement and public reporting of healthcare performance data that provide meaningful information about whether care is safe, timely, beneficial, patient-centered, equitable, and efficient."

The patient safety literature is so voluminous that it is easy to glide rapidly pass such pernicious pronouncements as these taken from the NQF self-description of what they will provide society:

- Clinically relevant guidelines that *may be used* by physicians—.

- Health care providers and other appropriate entities *may access or review*—.

- Will "improve American healthcare through endorsement of consensus-bases national standards for measurement and public reporting of healthcare performance data that provide meaningful information about whether care is safe or timely.

Am I the only person who can see *no* specific criterion should be anticipated to be forthcoming that will enable doctors to judge questionable patient care events? Guidelines that may be used to measure and review criteria, entities may access and consensus-bases national standards for measurement and public reporting do not promote confidence that real improvement in patient safety is eminent. Ten years after those prophetic words were written, the results are in, and needless hospital deaths continue to occur at the same tragic rate.

Agency for Healthcare Research and Quality (AHRQ) is one of the twelve agencies of DHHS, along with OIG-OEI and HCFA now CMS. AHRQ supports health services research initiatives that seek to improve the quality of health care in America and their mission is improve the quality, safety, efficiency, effectiveness, and cost-effectiveness of health care for all Americans.

Two examples of health services research initiatives are presented for consideration:

First, in 2002 NQF created and endorsed a list of serious reportable events (SREs) to increase public accountability and consumer access to critical information about healthcare performance. There are twenty-eight events, and each is classified under one of six categories: surgical, product or device, patient protection, care management, environment, or criminal.

Serious Reportable Events (SRE)
Surgical Events

- Surgery performed on the wrong body part.

- Surgery performed on the wrong person.

- Wrong surgical procedure performed on a patient.

- Unintended retention of a foreign object in a patient after surgery or other procedure.

- Intra-operative or immediately postoperative death in an ASA Class I patient. (i.e. a twenty-seven-year-old female for minor knee surgery under local anesthesia.)

Response: I completed my surgery residency training in 1966, and if memory serves me correctly, these five events were considered serious and reportable events long before that year. The sad fact is that for far too long, far too many serious, reportable surgical events have been either poorly reported or not reported at all.

More importantly, report the SRE to whom? And precisely what response should one anticipate? NQF's SREs are a cruel joke on society. If there had ever been a responsible source to report such events to, and if there had ever been a proven history of responsible action being taken, there would have been *no* need for NQF to have ever been created. Now, their cure for the problem is to offer vague national guidelines and standards devoid of specifics.

Secondly, NQF, with support from AHRQ, identified thirty safe practices that evidence shows can work to reduce or prevent adverse events and medical errors. A review of the direct patient safety impact of one of those thirty safe practices will demonstrate the relative value of nationally prescribed "standards."

Fact sheet: Thirty Safe Practices for Better Health Care (published by AHRQ March 2005).

Number 25: Decontaminate hands with either a hygienic hand rub or by washing with a disinfectant soap prior to, and after, direct contact with the patient or objects immediately around the patient.

History: Joseph Lister gets most of the credit for discovering the benefits of doctors washing their hands in 1865, but he freely gives credit, where credit is due, to the earlier work by Ignaz Semmelweis in Vienna. Semmelweis' proven research that doctors, by washing their hands, could save lives was harshly rejected by the medical leadership, first in Vienna and later in Budapest, because it would prove that doctors of that day had been needlessly killing far too many patients. According to Dr. John Clough, medical leadership continues to struggle with objectivity.

Local reality: The Greenville News, November 6, 2009: Hospitals work to scrub out infection: "It's a simple enough concept—wash your hands to reduce the spread of infection. But health care workers around the country only do it about half the time, according to the U.S. Centers for Disease Control and Prevention. Now, Greenville Hospital System University Medical Center wants to increase hand-washing compliance to 90 percent. Hand hygiene is critical to infection control. The three-year hand hygiene campaign will be comprised of awareness, education, and *account-ability*. In places that have done this well, it took three years to sustain 90 percent."

Summary: Semmelweis and Lister documented the patient safety value of doctors, and others, washing their hands over 150 years ago. AHRQ and NQF widely reinforced that safety standard in 2005. Four years later, the largest of the two hospital systems in Greenville, SC, are finally beginning a "three-year hand washing campaign of awareness, education and accountability." It appears that one word or thirty safe practices from the NQF and the rest of the health care Cottage Industry and hospital medical staffs do as they please, if they please.

Key word: Accountability. True accountability can only be developed, maintained, and properly utilized in an identifiable organizational structure. Unfortunately, such a vital element cannot be found in any segment of our current health care system, and nationally prescribed "standards" directed toward systems devoid of organizational structure are like shouting into the wind.

Institute of Medicine (IOM), a branch of National Academy of Science (NAS).

In 1996, IOM launched a concerted, ongoing effort focused on assessing and improving the nation's quality of care.

Crossing the Quality Chasm: The IOM Health Care Quality Initiative:

- *To Err Is Human: Building a Safer Health System (2000)*

- *Crossing the Quality Chasm: A New Health System for the 21st Century (2001)*

- *Leadership by Example: Coordinating Government Roles in Improving Health Care Quality (2002)*

- *Health Professions Education: A Bridge to Quality (2003)*

- *Priority Areas for National Action: Transforming Health Care Quality (2003)*

- *Patient Safety: Achieving a New Standard for Care: (2004)*

- *(Those 6 books contain a total of 53 Recommendations—See Appendix B)*

Response: Never before have so many highly educated, well-meaning individuals accumulated such a mass of bureaucratic nonsense intended primarily to empower themselves. Those seeking a cure for insomnia should attempt to read all fifty-three recommendations at one sitting. It would be interesting to run the entire contents of those six books though an adequate computer program to remove the enormous amount of redundancy and reduce the total number of books in half.

Challenge: Pick five of those fifty-three recommendations and show exactly how their implementation will provide direct patient care benefit in the approximately six thousand hospitals across our nation in the foreseeable future.

NQF has hundreds of members, including most Organized Medicine organizations, AHRQ, a division of DHHS which gives us JC oversight, shares accolades with NQF for recommending a 150-year-old standard that doctors should wash their hands, and IOM mass produces a series of books containing esoteric recommendations promising that given enough time, those experts on high will cure all that ails questionable patient care.

Seemingly, almost everyone in the health care cottage industry is on the same page, and apparently no one is asking, "Are we going in the right direction?" The problems affecting our health care system are too great to permit any group, association, or governmental agency to be considered above reproach. While some may view these comments offensive, our current health care chaos requires an open debate. It will be interesting to see if such an open debate will take place.

Doctors

Self-denial: Doctors forgot who "they" are and what they intended to be to and for society. Doctors were meant to serve the public, and in our lifetime the practice of medicine (like driving a car) is a *privilege* granted by the state.

What went wrong with doctors is not as complicated as it may seem. We need to remember that doctors are only human, and all humans make mistakes. Plus, most doctors are, at best, average practitioners within the whole. Therefore, questionable patient care will happen in every community from time to time with every doctor, though some more often than most.

Doctors are the best judge(s) of other doctors, But doctors don't know how to judge other doctors.

Two generalities of questionable patient care:

* A doctor assumes responsibility to provide medical treatment for patient care that they are not qualified to render.

* A doctor assumes responsibility to provide medical treatment for patient care they are qualified to render but skips a step or makes a human error, which results in harm to the patient.

What went wrong with doctors is their inability to properly differentiate between those two significantly different types of questionable patient care.

Every form of questionable patient care review

revolves around the medical standard of care of that specific form of treatment.

The truth about the medical standard of care:

Every medical procedure, from the removal of ingrown toenails to open-heart surgery (I've had both), has its own, specific standard of care. Equally important, that standard of care is specific to the practitioner treating the patient, and it is *not* a well-researched imagination created by some far-removed, quality-care impresario.

Would any person in their right mind permit a doctor to perform major surgery knowing beforehand that practitioner is unable to articulate their personal standard of care for that planned surgery? Patients do it every day throughout the nation.

There is a reality of medical care largely unrecognized by NQF, AHRQ, IOM, and the rest of the health care cottage industry. That reality requires an understanding of the medical standard of care, the art and the science of medicine, turf wars, out-dated medical treatment and the real cost of the absence of effective medical peer review within every hospital medical staff. A good starting point is with the medical dilemma.

Medical Dilemma: There are only two routinely functional systems having the "potential" to review questionable patient care—malpractice litigation and medical peer review. The result is that 99.9 percent of all questionable patient care has either been reviewed through the malpractice litigation system (far too few) or never reviewed at all.

The cause of that dilemma is that doctors themselves have never been able to clearly define the medical standard of care for even the most simple of medical procedures. The medical standard of care has two inherent characteristics—art and science—and their inability to define the standard of care is due to their inability to ever be able to identify, define, and judge the *art* of medicine.

The Art and Science of all medical care: The perfect analogy for the practice of medicine is a pilot flying a single engine airplane. Each student pilot is taught the science of flying an airplane. Each pilot, student or graduate, provides their personal art of flying an airplane each time they take off and hopefully land safely. The exact same combination of science and art occurs each and every time a doctor treats a patient.

All medical care has three inherent characteristics: science, art, and a standard of care.

Science of Medicine: Doctors are taught the science of medicine. Medical schools transform non-doctors into doctors. Other than rare exceptions, all current medical care has a scientific basis derived from previous forms of medical care.

Art of Medicine: The art of medicine has always existed. Every doctor provides their personal art to each patient they treat. From a tonsillectomy to a heart transplant, each patient is like a painter's fresh canvas, where the doctors practice their art of medicine. But no doctor can tell you exactly what it is or how to find and judge it.

Dr. Audiey Kao, AMA Vice President, Ethics Standards, said in 2002, "A not-so-famous man once said, 'If you can't measure it, it's less likely to be important.' In the case of good medicine, it is widely accepted that we need to measure how well physicians are providing clinical care so that we can continue to make improvements. I would agree that this logic applies not only to the science of medicine, but also in many important respects to the art of medicine—otherwise it simply becomes *idealistic rhetoric* (emphasis added). Leaders in medicine must work together to develop effective ways of imparting and evaluating the ethical skills and competencies of physicians."

Though the medical profession has failed to establish a means of identifying, defining, and judging one of the two inherent characteristics of all medical care, it does not mean the art of medicine is intangible, unidentifiable, or incapable of being judged. I wrote Dr. Kao that I can identify, define, and judge the art of medicine in late 2004, along with a copy of my first book: *First, Do No Harm, The Cure for Medical Malpractice.* I never heard from the good doctor.

A doctor cannot treat a patient in any manner without that treatment having a standard of care composed of medical science and that doctor's personal art of medicine.

The phrase "medical standard of care" is probably more used and less understood than any other phrase in medical literature. Some hospitals advertise "treatment to a higher standard," when their medical staff cannot even define the previous standard of care. Health care cottage industry fills their literature with buzz words (standards, quality, standard of care) without the ability to truly define them in terms of basic medical care: one doctor, one patient.

Standard is defined as a rule used as a basis for judgment. Standard, the word, is used copiously throughout the quality of health care literature, but unfortunately, the standards so readily spoken and written of are not and cannot ever be used to actually judge the quality of questionable patient care. Therefore, any standard lacking the ability to be used as a basis for judgment is a false promise to those who are presumed to be the target audience. The South Carolina Hospital Association (SCHA) recently provided a perfect example of the perfidious use of the word standard on their Web site with the following pronouncement:

"The Joint Commission sets the standards by which health care quality is measured and evaluates the quality and safety of care for nearly 17,000 health care organizations." At my request, the current president of the SCHA read that statement and responded, "That's a lie!" I said, "I know and that is why I wanted you to read it." That statement regarding The Joint Commission is no longer on the SCHA

Web site. The purposeful misuse of the word standard has become so pervasive throughout the health care literature that the true meaning of that word has been lost, hopefully not forever.

Fifty years ago, Organized Medicine publicly vowed that doctors would set their own standard(s) of care. Now, medical malpractice is treatment beneath a standard of care "set by the law." Still, the AMA continues to proclaim their concern for their patients while failing to explain that great leap backward from doctors judging patient care to "sue or forget it."

The medical standard of care was made "indefinable" at the same time the medical profession chose malpractice litigation to be the principle system for the review of questionable patient care.

Turf Wars: Specialization of the practice of medicine, a boon to rapidly advancing technologies, has also resulted in patients euphemistically being thought of as body parts. A byproduct of specialization is that several different medical specialties are qualified to treat the same conditions. This creates turf wars.

Ear, nose, and throat doctors, plastic surgeons, and oral surgeons all typically have hospital privileges to treat jaw fractures. Orthopedic and neurosurgery practitioners compete over back surgery cases, and orthopedic and plastic surgeons compete over hand surgery cases. The list is long and varies with individual hospital medical staffs.

There can be a wide variation between the qualifications and abilities of the individual practitioners in competing specialties. Rarely are those discrepancies properly addressed. Regardless of whether a community has one or several hospitals, hospital medical staff leaders have an ethical obligation to their community. They must recognize only those practitioners who are *best qualified* to provide a *current* and *acceptable* standard of care and limit the less qualified, regardless of specialty. But then, turf wars are seldom discussed.

Outdated Forms of Medical Care: The use of outdated forms of medical care, if identifiable, would easily be the greatest source of questionable patient care events. Doctors practice for decades, and medical technology is consistently changing. Therefore, a gap in each practitioner's ability to remain *current* in all aspects of their personal medical specialty is inevitable. The quality of medicine problem is that the medical profession has made little attempt to directly deal with that inevitability, while the malpractice litigation system has perpetuated it. Hospitals that advertise various treatments to a "higher standard" are unknowingly advertising that a technological gap must exist within their current medical staff, and that gap will remain hidden.

The South Carolina Medical Association published a *Physician's Guide to Malpractice Law in South Carolina, updated in March 2000.* That guide contains a ten-page charge to the jury, given by a judge in 1999. One brief quote will illustrate how courts deal with turf wars and outdated forms of treatment: "Where there is more than one recognized diagnosis or treatment, and not one of them is used exclusively and uniformly by all practitioners in good standing, it is not negligence for a doctor if, in exercising his best judgment, he selects one of the approved methods, which later turns out to be a wrong selection or one not favored by certain other practitioners. In short, it is quite possible for a physician to be unsuccessful in his treatment or to disagree with others of his profession without being negligent."

Thus, a quality of care "perfect storm" is created when elements of turf wars, outdated forms of treatment, and legally acceptable standards of care set at the lowest possible hurdle come together in the crucible of medical malpractice litigation.

Who better to tell how bad things really are within one medical specialty than the doctors themselves? Obstetricians have been the poster child for AMA in their endless quest for medical malpractice tort reform (tort reform is the legislative transfer of patient's rights to the benefit of doctors and has zero benefit toward improving the questionable patient care problem and will be examined in more detail in the chapter "Other Offerings").

Peer Review in Obstetrics and Gynecology by a National Medical Specialty Society: Joint Commission Journal on Quality and Safety, February 2003.

"Peer review is the cornerstone of any effective program for medical quality assessment."

"American College of Obstetricians and Gynecologists (ACOG) established the Voluntary Review of Quality Care (VRQC) program in 1986. Over the next 16 years, 193 site visits were conducted, which represented 6% of the 3,003 hospitals which reported providing obstetric inpatient care. VRQC program is voluntary, confidential and has no regulatory authority to sanction, accredit, or grant licensure.

"The first 100 site visits took place in 29 states and represented a diverse geographic cohort of hospital departments of obstetrics and gynecology. Overall departmental and systemic deficiencies were significantly more common than clinical concerns. In very large departments, a representative sample of physicians is reviewed, including those with the highest volume of the procedure under study, as well as potentially poor-quality practitioners *previously identified* by the hospital. Within the context of the VRQC program, the term *deficiency* is used to indicate departures from commonly accepted medical practice, but not necessarily substandard care. Areas of deficiency identified were grouped into three categories, Obstetric, Gynecologic and Systemic. Systemic deficiencies included, credentialing/privileging, disruptive physician and 'turf battles.'"

Table 3. System Deficiencies Found in the First 100 Site Visits:

DEFICIENCY	NO. OF HOSPITALS IDENTIFIED
Lack of effective peer review	84
Poor documentation	77
Lack of continuing medical education	68
Poor privileging and credentialing	67
Poor policy and procedures	59
Substandard or disruptive physician(s)	38

"The VRQC program, as a voluntary consultative peer preview program, addresses hospital-specific quality problems and also identifies common deficiencies across a diverse group of hospitals, which may warrant continuing education."

Two additional items of note:

ACOG and American Society of Anesthesiologists (ASA) are the only two of the twenty-four recognized medical specialties conducting such peer review programs as of 2003.

"Some of the hospitals were seeking remediation for problem-prone physicians within their facilities, but because of the difficulty in finding "mini-residencies" for such physicians, the VRQC program was limited in its ability to offer substantive recommendations for external retraining efforts."

I, acting solely, organized the first "mini-residency" ever held in oral and maxillofacial surgery for the surgical correction of jaw deformities in Madison, Wisconsin, in 1970. The mini-residency method of advanced training for practicing surgeons became a common event in oral and maxillofacial surgery throughout the country shortly after. Yet, thirty years later, ACOG decries having no such remedial training opportunities for their members, while loudly complaining that their only salvation can come from medical malpractice tort reform and acknowledging that they and the ASA are the only two medical specialties out of twenty-four that had made any attempt at peer review within their respected associations.

Also of note, the author of that journal article, and a principle in the creation of the ACOG's VRQC program, is the source of the most recent public announcement that after twenty years of effort, "2,000 needless hospital deaths per week continue to occur in our nation." Therefore, if it was an estimated 98,000 needless hospital deaths per year in 1990, then the current 104,000 needless hospital deaths per year signify patient safety is going in the wrong direction."

And doctors wonder, "What went wrong?"

Summary

Organized medicine: Chose medical malpractice litigation over medical peer review.

States: Failed to recognize their obligation for the regulation and control of the private practice of medicine and of hospital medical staffs, and that failure continues in every state today.

Federal: Blurred the lines of authority, responsibility, and accountability along with introducing JC hospital certification for Medicare with *no* real oversight, a NPDB system that is basically worthless, and a PRO/QIO system of medical peer review that functions as a sub-standard bookkeeper.

Joint Commission: Accepted the free gift of hospital certification for Medicare from Congress and turned that responsibility into a regulatory sham.

Cottage Industry: Changed into a monolithic system attempting to create quality patient care by proclamations from on high orchestrated through federal agencies.

Doctors: Abdicated their professional responsibility of regulation and control of their members to the legal profession and continue to wonder, "What went wrong?"

Patient Safety Activists should reread the Peer Review in Obstetrics and Gynecology segment and then compare that to:

- NQF/AHRQ 30 Points and SREs.

- IOM Crossing the Quality Chasm fifty-three recommendations.

- DHHS 1999 oversight review of JC.

- JC Medical Staff Handbook, which renames medical peer review and gives it 1/336 of the entire manual.

Which of those illustrations best depicts the reality found within a hospital medical staff near you? Those governmental and professional organizations comprise a very large portion of the mass of people who are currently planning on changing your health care system in the very near future.

Perhaps the analogy of the development of our nation's health care system being far too similar to Darwin's theory of evolution is beginning to resonate. Our health care system is severely flawed, and those flaws, both cost and organizational structure deserve much more consideration than is being discussed by all parties involved in planning that future change.

WHAT WENT RIGHT?

Organizationally speaking, it is difficult to imagine that anything meaningful has taken place within our health care system that could be worthy of note; but several positive events have occurred in the past. More importantly, two of those positive events have produced a Jekyll and Hyde response within the medical profession by creating enormously positive improvements in practitioners' credentialing and patient safety, while at the same time being greeted within that profession with the ardor offered an illegitimate child.

Organized Medicine specifically, and all other components of health care generally, have not only failed to create a health care system one could be proud of, they have callously turned their backs on the few real events that might have opened the door for a health care system far more beneficial to all.

Three events will be used in chronologically reverse order to illustrate that things sometimes do go right in health care, but the response to positive health care events is not always as those events deserve.

First Event: VA Health System Rejuvenation. Dr. Kenneth Kizer, Under Secretary for Health in the VA from 1994–1999, is widely credited with being the chief architect of the VA's remarkable transformation from a system-wide state of disarray to the far more acceptable status it enjoys today. The VA system, source of my internship and three-year surgery residency, had fallen on hard times; and Dr. Kizer, while not acting alone, is given most of the credit for the VA's quality of care resurrection.

Information technology (IT) was one of the principle tools Dr. Kizer and others used for the VA's rapid rejuvenation, and IT is what makes this event worthy of consideration, because IT plays such an important part in the current debate regarding health care change in America. If one were to Google "health care infrastructure," as I have done, the major portion of the thousands of responses would be focused on IT.

Information technology is *not* an element of our health care system's organizational infrastructure, in spite of its current importance in the function of modern health care. To equate IT with the health care organizational infrastructure is to create further confusion in a currently existing debate rife with confusion. Such misuse of IT serves only as a plea for the use of precise nomenclature of health care change. Prior to this book, no one has even attempted to describe the organizational infrastructure of our health care system and now, to add distortion of terms to an essential part of what should be a part of the health care debate only adds more confusion. IT will be part of the final consideration for how to change our health care system, but IT is not, and will not, be found to be a part of that system's organizational infrastructure. Our current culture, with its sound-bit mentality, is hyper-susceptible to losing sight of how to use precise terms for significant issues.

Dr. Kizer went from the VA to be the first President and CEO of NQF from 1999 to 2006. Now, to far more important positive events in health care that have, for the most part, been carelessly ignored, much to society's detriment.

Public notice of the second event of what went right in health care first came to my notice with an article in the local Madison, Wisconsin, newspaper.

Second Event: Department of Defense External Civilian Peer Review of Medical Care. Wisconsin State Journal, October 1987: Military Health Care Passes Test: "The Pentagon instituted a sophisticated peer review system to document the quality of care delivered in military hospitals. And based on initial results, it appears that military physicians are stacking up favorably against their civilian counterparts. *The Pentagon cannot be sure, however, because it discovered the private sector lacks a standardized system for reviewing the work of doctors on high-risk cases as sophisticated as that created by the military.*" (Organized Medicine continues to lack such a system as of 2009.)

Just one year later, those doctors who read the JAMA became aware of what the Department of Defense had accomplished.

JAMA, November 1988: A First Report of the Department of Defense External Civilian Peer Review of Medical Care: (Note the two significant elements contained in that title: it speaks of a system of peer review created by civilian physicians).

"In mid-1985, the Department of Defense announced a plan for an external civilian peer review of selected medical and surgical cases in military hospitals. In early 1986, the Department of Defense initiated a bold activity. The review, by civilian physicians external to the military, of the quality of medical care in the hospitals of the US Army, US Navy and US Air Force. The health care services available to approximately nine million Department of Defense beneficiaries are provided in 168 hospitals plus approximately 500 free-standing clinics."

Among these Department of Defense initiatives were a validation and review of the credentials of physicians, development of criteria for granting clinical privileges, establishment of a licensing requirement for physicians, and the development of hospital-cased, computer-assisted quality assurance programs that focused on the monitoring and evaluation of both medical events and health care providers.

Review of the literature soon confirmed that nationally accepted medical care standards and criteria rarely existed for the types of diagnoses that were of interest to the Department of Defense. The magnitude of this review process, employing uniform standards and an enormous volume of data, is unprecedented. Traditional methods were coupled with modern technology to allow maximum use of computer analysis and highly focused review by the peer review panel of practicing physicians.

Some of the positive factors gained from this new (back then) system of peer review were:

- Creation of a sophisticated peer review system.

- Documented quality of care.

- Validation and review of the credentials of physicians.

- Development of criteria for granting clinical privileges.

- Established a licensing requirement.

- Computer assisted quality assurance program that focused on the monitoring and evaluation of both medical events and health care providers.

- Demonstrated how the private sector lacks a standardized system.

Surely that is a very impressive list of highly desirable characteristics in medical care, right? But what was Organized Medicine's response to that innovative accomplishment, which took two years to even appear in the JAMA?

JAMA November 1988: Assessing Quality: John T. Kelly, MD, Ph.D., AMA: "The Department of Defense has established an innovative system to evaluate and improve the quality of care provided to Department of Defense beneficiaries. Their system is particularly noteworthy because it illustrates the likely direction for evolution in quality assessment systems. They have shown that objective review criteria can be established, that computers can be used effectively to assist quality assessment efforts and that review of case abstracts can substitute for medical record review. The approach used by the Department of Defense is likely to diffuse throughout the medical care system because it has the potential to facilitate peer review that is more objective and cost-effective."

Two Decades Later: Those deeply committed to helping create a far better health care system should thoroughly read and understand that JAMA article of 1988 describing the efforts established by the Department of Defense *and* the AMA response immediately following that article. Over twenty years later, Dr. Kelly's prediction that the Department of Defense efforts in medical peer review will be "likely to diffuse throughout the medical care system" have proven to be tragically accurate, when one understands that the definition of diffuse is to scatter widely or thinly. While the Department of Defense innovations in practitioner credentialing and peer review have been diffusing widely and thinly, the rate of needless hospital deaths has also remained unchanged during those same past twenty years.

I met with the person who administers the credentialing of every doctor and dentist in the Navy in 2004, shortly after my book, *First, Do No Harm, The Cure for Medical Malpractice,* was published. Because that person had complete understanding of the credentialing and peer review of practitioners and patient care, we were able to discuss in great detail the system of medical peer review I advocate. Within one hour, that person's last comment to me was, "Dr. Williams, I see your system, and it is so simple."

Five years later, all of those who have been actively engaged in attempting to improve the quality of health care in America have refused to consider my system of medical peer review and compare it to any and all other methods of how to better judge questionable patient care. Wide and thin diffusion of ways to better judge the quality of health care, and the review of questionable patient care is continuing to cost far too many needless hospital deaths.

The third event has two characteristics that should demand great consideration. This event represents what I would argue is one of the most important articles in all of medical literature in the last three decades, and at the same time it is one of the most ignored. Legions of experts at Harvard search for ways to improve the quality of patient care while pretending that a perfect example of rapid patient care improvement did not take place at their own institution. Readers must judge for themselves.

Third Event: Harvard Anesthesia Department Minimum Standards: JAMA August 1986: Standards for Patient Monitoring During Anesthesia at Harvard Medical School:

Harvard is self-insured and has its own risk management organization. Even so, Harvard Medical School was not spared as the second wave of the medical malpractice crisis cycled through our nation in the early 1980s. Particularly noteworthy to the Harvard risk management department was the costly impact of the Medical School's Anesthesia Department.

That department's leadership was told, "You must do something to greatly improve your present rate of medical liability." And to that department's credit they did do something quick and dramatic. The Harvard Medical School Department of Anesthesia controlled nine separate departments at nine separate hospitals within their system. A committee was formed, and the past patient care incidents were studied to gain an understanding of where the greatest cause(s) of those incidents occurred. Their findings showed that basic patient monitoring practices were thought to be so important in accident prevention that they must become mandatory. *The creation of mandatory basic monitoring guidelines in the practice of medicine had never been done before.*

The Harvard Medical School Department of Anesthesia devised seven specific, detailed, mandatory standards for minimal patient monitoring during anesthesia at its nine component teaching hospitals. *I see those minimal standards like seven lines drawn in the sand that said to every department anesthesiologist, "Doctor, if you cross one of those lines, we can* not *help you."* By going where no other medical organization had ever gone before, they became professional heretics.

A brief description of those seven minimal standards of patient monitoring during anesthesia were:

1. Anesthesiologist/nurse anesthetist present in OR.*

2. Blood pressure and heart rate @ 5 minutes.*

3. Electrocardiogram.

4. Continuous monitoring (ventilation and circulation).*

5. Breathing system disconnection monitoring.

6. Oxygen analyzer.

7. Measure temperature (malignant hyperthermia).

Individually and collectively, none of those minimal standards appear to be asking too much of a dedicated anesthesiologist. Harvard risk management got the quick and dramatic result they were seeking. Within one year, the medical liability rate for that anesthesia department showed a wonderful improvement. But improved quality patient care is not the perspective taken by Organized Medicine.

Harvard's view of their new, minimum standards: "As part of a major patient safety/risk management effort, the Department of Anesthesia of Harvard Medical School, Boston has devised specific, detailed, mandatory standards for minimal patient monitoring during anesthesia at its nine component teaching hospitals. *They are fundamental, minimal standards that would be achievable in the smallest rural community hospital.* Such standards had not previously existed and resistance to the concept was anticipated, but not seen. Physicians have traditionally resisted standards of practice that dictate their day-to-day conduct of medical care."

Organized Medicine's view of those standards: JAMA August 1986 (response to the original article and immediately following): "The opportunity for self-determination, for being one's own boss, has been for many of us one of the pluses of being a physician. As such, it is presented not so much to enlighten JAMA readership concerning monitoring as one aspect of anesthesia care, but as an example of a process for extracting a collective minimum standard from individuals long accustomed to defining their own destiny and unaccustomed to others telling them what they should do. The essence of our role as problem-solving givers of care is independent thought and action. Anything that appears to constrain that freedom will be viewed as threatening one's ability to provide care in the way each of us believe to be the best. We are being provoked to be accountable for both the costs and benefits of our care."

My view of those standards: I was taught the three minimal standards that are noted in the list above by the asterisks (*) in 1963, and the other four minimal standards represent technological advancements. Malignant hyperthermia became a recognized anesthesia hazard in the mid to late 1970s.

Harvard risk management view of those standards: Joyful shock at the positive and rapid results of such simple, "mandatory minimums" in patient care and safety.

Wisconsin State Journal, December 1986: "A majority of anesthesia deaths are malpractice. As many as 75% of the 2,000 or more anesthesia deaths are the result of malpractice. Fourteen percent of 624 cases studied involved failure to maintain the patient's airway open."

Now think about this: In Madison, Wisconsin, in the mid '70s, a middle-aged wife and mother had a D&C under general anesthesia as the University of Wisconsin hockey team was playing in the NCAA final four on television. *When her anesthesiologist went down the hall to watch the game, her breathing tube disconnected, and she became brain dead.* As Harvard Medical School Department of Anesthesia overview stated, "They are fundamental, minimal standards that would be achievable in the smallest community hospital." The above tragedy occurred in the largest hospital in Madison.

Now reread Organized Medicine's response to how those minimal standards were looked at as a threat to the freedom of doing their work as "they thought best." Assume the organization of airline pilots was responding in a like manner to operational restrictions being placed upon their performance. Would such a professional response cause concern from that source?

What if the three Harvard minimal standards of 1986—that I had been taught in 1963—had been minimal standards in every hospital in America during those years? Think of the tragedies that would have been averted by even "three lines in the sand" for all anesthesiologists. That woman in Madison, her family and her anesthesiologist would not have been forced to face that life-altering event, and that is just one example of what is now euphemistically called *never events.*

Yet after the initial negative response to the original JAMA article, and a few additional negative letters to the editor, there was silence from the leaders of Organized Medicine. There was no bandwagon to jump on. Organized Medicine was left with the Harvard Medical School Department of Anesthesia "heretics."

If others view, as I do, the DoD and Harvard Anesthesia Department events to be extremely positive steps in patient safety and improved quality of health care, then much can be gained from a retrospective study of those events and the response(s) to them. The initial response from within Organized Medicine was included from the JAMA. Far more telling responses can be obtained, if sought.

The Harvard Anesthesia Department event demonstrated rapid and dramatic patient safety improvement by using *"a few fundamental, minimal standards that would be achievable in the smallest community hospital."* That achievement occurred over twenty years ago.

Harvard School of Public Health has long been a major source of nationally recognized leaders collaborating in the production of volumes of literature related to patient safety and quality health care issues. Search the patient safety and quality health care literature seeking *any* references to the DoD and Harvard Anesthesia Department events, but anticipate finding few such references—if any. Positive patient safety efforts ignored should be considered worse than making no efforts whatsoever to improve patient safety.

IOM Crossing the *Quality Chasm* series, AHRQ/ NQF 30 Points, and the latest efforts through the NQF National Priorities Partnership are models for improving patient safety and quality health care using guidelines and standards formulated by experts far removed from the site of questionable patient care and utilizing "systems cures" based within "non-punitive environments."

The system of hospital medical staff peer review

presented later in this book is based upon doctors fairly judging other doctors rapidly and at the site of the questionable patient care. Harvard Anesthesia Department long ago proved the dramatic value of such a patient safety reform while using only a very few minimum standards.

Patient safety activists should ask themselves, "Which method of improved patient safety best offers the quality health care changes I am seeking at the hospital medical staff nearest me?"

Perhaps even more distressing should be the scarcity of positive patient safety events to be found in the medical literature. The Harvard Medical School Department of Anesthesia minimum standards with their rapid and greatly beneficial result should have become a beacon of light in the quest for greater patient safety. Try to find those who have even heard about it enough to retain its value.

All health care is local, and the Harvard Anesthesia Department proved—I say again—they proved that the regulation of medical practice applied at the local level will provide the most rapid and effective results. Compare the Harvard results to the current health care cottage industry results of sanctimonious, non-specific guidelines for greater patient safety that in ten years have yielded no evidence of benefit to society at the hospital medical staff level of the hospital nearest you.

Authority, responsibility, and most important of

all, accountability, *must* function within every hospital medical staff in the nation, but those critical elements *must* have a clearly defined organizational structure before they can function properly. Far too many people continue to die needlessly in our hospitals in spite of monumental efforts by so many, while everyone continues to look for solutions that are meant to "trickle down from on high."

HOW TO FIX IT

Health care change is currently assumed to soon be accomplished through Cost and Access change, with information technology added. Sadly, that is another political pipedream.

Cost and access health care change, combined with huge inclusions of information technology throughout the system, will be like that time worn bromide, rearranging the deck chairs on the Titanic. Unfortunately in this case, that time worn bromide is an accurate description of the present state of affairs. Our health care ship is also fatally gashed as it is currently structured and its salvation requires much more than cost and access change alone.

Truly beneficial health care change would include cost and access change with:

- Understanding of its present organizational configuration, including all essential parts.

- Fundamental restructuring with clearly defined

points of *authority, responsibility,* and *accountability* (all sorely missing essentials).

(Abraham Flexner, one hundred years ago, first began his study by describing the historical evolution of that subject he was to recommend changes for, medical education.)

Three recommendations are offered as a first-step basis for fundamental health care change. The first recommendation, which is needed as rapidly as possible, will be an integral part of describing the historical evolution of health care in America. The second recommendation can also be quickly accomplished so as to become an important asset to the same task.

The third recommendation is the most important missing link in our current health care system. Far too many patients are needlessly harmed daily across America because all of the states have failed to recognize their *absolute* responsibility to regulate the private practice of medicine, hospital medical staffs, and now, freestanding surgery centers. Yet no state has ever recognized this responsibility or shown the slightest remorse for their indefensible lapse of authority that has led to such human tragedy.

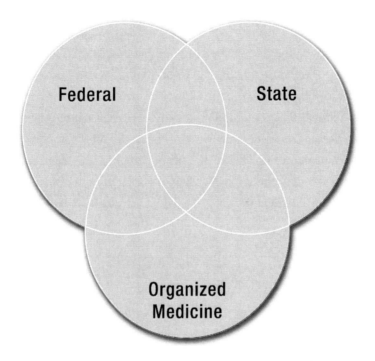

Federal

State

Organized
Medicine

First Recommendation: Un-blur the lines of authority. Easier said than done, but still an absolute necessity.

Look again at the Major Components design, and strive to envision the points of *authority, responsibility,* and *accountability.* The question, "Where should one begin?" will illustrate the magnitude of such a quest, followed, hopefully, by the realization that this indispensable social institution is a vast administrative quagmire.

Health care in America is federal involvement through Medicare and Medicaid, managed care and insurance coverage, and all of the rest of the relatively new attempts at managing segments of the whole—*but*—the basic core of health care is now, and always will be, one doctor treating one patient.

Therefore, the first question that *must* be asked and answered, without equivocation is, do states, and states alone, possess the final authority over the private practice of medicine and hospital medical staffs? No clear understanding of health care in America can ever be achieved without clarification of that seminal point.

Medical equation:

- Most medical schools are state-run institutions, therefore states regulate medical education

- Most newly graduated doctors must get a state license to practice medicine; therefore, states regulate the licensing of medical doctors

- Most hospitals are state regulated, therefore since states:
    -Regulate medical education
    -License doctors to practice medicine
    -Regulate most hospitals

- Then states are responsible for the regulation of:
    -Medical practice
    -Hospital medical staffs
    -Surgery centers

South Carolina's two medical schools graduated classes of new doctors in May 2009 and I asked my state legislator, "What is one of the first things those new doctors must do?" He replied. "I guess get a job." "No! They must first get a state license to practice medicine. Therefore who has the responsibility to regulate the private practice of medicine, hospital medical staffs and the seldom spoken-of surgery clinics?"

And none of the fifty states have a clue regarding the *regulatory mechanism* they and their citizens *presume* has been created. While the federal government is continuing to appropriate more and more control over the entire health care system, no recognition is given to this fundamental fact by anyone at any level of government. States have long had this responsibility that is apparently oblivious to everyone taking part in future health care change. Too often the obvious becomes obscure, and often to the detriment of all.

Federal, state, Organized Medicine, and the JC must be required to clearly describe their specific contribution to the whole system, including the points of authority, responsibility, and accountability within their respective purview. Fulfillment of this task by each of the health care components will be an educational experience in itself. It's often very interesting to watch agencies in authority attempt to describe the source and utilization of that authority.

Such a joint process, should it ever take place, will rapidly expose the hubris of health care change limited to cost and access and information technology (IT). Health care charlatans promising health care change by quibbling over the innumerable ways to divide that system's financial pie is a repeat of the cruel promise of what federal participation would do for education in America.

Understanding: A simple request for the various components of health care to clarify their respective lines of authority *should not* create consternation and chaos; but regarding health care it will—bet on it. The more difficult that process becomes, the more clearly its need will become evident. It will also be interesting to see how the dialogue at health care meetings would change during the process of un-blurring the health care lines of authority.

Lastly, the process of un-blurring the lines of authority, responsibility, and accountability will expose the absence of such a need being evident within the voluminous cottage industry guidelines for quality health care. Six of the seven IOM's *Crossing the Quality Chasm* books contain fifty-three recommendations for improving the quality of patient care throughout the health care system and the last of those six books was published in 2004. A true test of the value of that great literary undertaking would be to determine how many of those fifty-three recommendations have made a measurable improvement in patient safety at a hospital near you. Our health care system is drowning in a sea of theoretical babble, and order can only be obtained through a clearly defined organizational infrastructure—the most important ingredient missing in our health care system today.

I very recently had the good fortune to meet a newly selected member of the IOM and told him of my strong misgivings regarding that entire series and its highly nebulous recommendations. I challenged that well-positioned health care authority to demonstrate how transparent the IOM will choose to be by defending their highly acclaimed and equally questionable large body of literature. Time will tell if the IOM welcomes and responds openly to such a request.

One must compare the rapid and positive patient safety results achieved by the Harvard Anesthesia Department's minimum standards of care established at the point of care to the lack of evidence of greater patient safety stemming from the IOM's *Crossing the Quality Chasm* series of books after five years and at a hospital medical staff near you. See Appendix B.

Second recommendation: Czar: The White House has so marginalized the use of the term czar, but for lack of a better title, *czar* will be used here but with far different intent. States should create a health care czar office that will *not* become a bureaucracy and will have *no* authority to create regulation, but complete authority to obtain information from every source of health care within that state and responsibility to coordinate response to health care concerns.

Example: Each state should be required to collect

and organize every law, act, and statute, etc. which has contributed to creating their current health care system of regulation. (Flexner's model.) During that process it would be highly educational to see how many different people necessary to accomplish that task and how long it would take.

Each state should have a person who could say, "I can provide all of that information rapidly." Health care is one of the most important aspects of our society and one of the least understood. Reason: No one has ever taken the time to organize a state's health care system under one roof.

Example: A recent, sad story that exposes a lot of what is wrong in our health care system today concerns an older doctor near Fort Worth, Texas, who became a specialist in treating chronic pain and over several years built up a practice of about three hundred patients.

A woman patient and her divorce attorney filed a complaint against this doctor for an issue not of the doctor's making that led to the doctor's license being suspended by the Texas Medical Board. The woman later recanted her questionable complaint, but without effect on the Texas Medical Board.

The doctor, his practice, and his patients have been in suspension limbo for over two years, during which time four of the doctor's patients have killed themselves due to their untreated pain. Governor Rick Perry, the state attorney general, legislators, and newspapers have gotten involved to some degree, but the Texas Medical Board hasn't acted.

Does anyone see the real problem here? Chronic pain treatment has always been one of the areas of medicine that is more mystery than fact. Few doctors have a strongly based understanding of that malady and prescribing narcotics is fraught with regulatory danger.

State medical examining boards should be the last place any state official should turn to and expect rapid and concise response.

Texas has seven medical schools and numerous teaching hospitals. Somewhere in that plethora of highest medical knowledge some small group of medical educators should be able to provide chronic pain medication guidelines that meet current understanding regarding the acceptable use of narcotics.

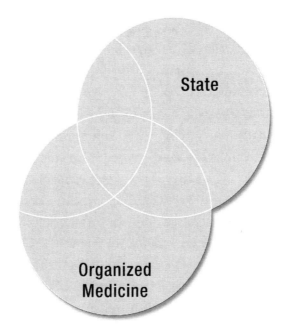

Look now at just the relationship between the State and Organized Medicine components, and strive to envision the vast quantity of medical expertise captured within the overlapped segments. There is an enormous amount of *un-harnessed* medical knowledge and *no* means to properly utilize it. A Texas health care czar could more rapidly deal with that chronic pain care physician's dilemma than that state's slow-as-molasses medical examining board and in a far more effective manner. What good is medical expertise if you are unable to fully utilize it? People need to demand more from their state legislatures regarding the regulation and control of the practice of medicine.

What was Southwestern America like prior to the Hoover (Boulder) Dam? Unharnessed power (knowledge) is both a waste and a drain on the fundamentals of any society. Every state in America has been sitting on an ignored and untapped medical resource while lamenting their woeful health care system.

Health care czar to the rescue: Every state has an ample supply of medical expertise in or near their borders. Every state has several medical quandaries perplexing numerous people. No state has a means for harnessing their medical expertise in order to create acceptable solutions in such cases as that doctor and his patients near Fort Worth, Texas.

A state health care czar, with sufficient authority to get medical information rapidly and concisely, would greatly increase the full utilization of all of that medical expertise currently functioning in a diverse and uncoordinated manner. Medical expertise is of little value unless you can use it, and we have always greatly underutilized ours.

Conundrum: State medical schools and teaching hospitals are constantly training new physicians in the "art" of current and acceptable standards of care in every form of medical specialty, while each state has numerous hospitals where medical practitioners are treating patients using out-dated techniques on a daily basis, and "medical experts" joust in civil court rooms over how to clearly describe the "standard of care" that best suits their side of the legal question for marginally educated lay jurors.

And *every* state has tolerated this supreme lack of rational thinking throughout the history of health care in America. Don't people deserve better? Quality of effort can never make up for the lack of definitive organizational understanding. The extreme lack of such understanding and coordination of effort has been crippling our health care system throughout its history.

The two brief examples given with the second recommendation are only very small examples of what a properly functional state health care czar (I fear the value of that term has become so tarnished as to possibly be useless, unfortunately) can provide by harnessing the medical expertise every state currently allows to go to waste. Given an opportunity, I can help those seeking the benefits of such an effort to flesh out the wide potential an office of that type can deliver because the potential benefits go far beyond the limited example offered here. Most states have one or more medical schools and/or teaching hospitals that have an enormous amount of un-harnessed medical expertise and too many of their citizens are needlessly suffering due to that fact.

There *must* be a better way, and there is!

The Third Recommendation to be offered is the "magic bullet" necessary to kill the quality health care beast and finally cross the quality chasm. When confronted with the alarming fact that no real progress has been made after twenty years of effort to reduce the 98,000 needless hospital deaths annually, (or is it now, as one medical expert recently put it, 104,000 needless hospital deaths annually) one should consider that, perhaps, those past efforts have been looking for a solution in the wrong direction.

As America's early medical profession transformed itself into what is now known as Organized Medicine, it faced a Sophia's choice: Which system of questionable patient care review should be allowed to become dominate—medical peer review or medical malpractice litigation? Unfortunately for all, they passively chose the latter.

If one reads the AMA Leadership's pronouncements contained in the JAMA during the 1950s and

'60s (as I have done), they will see that our medical profession recognized:

- Doctors are the best judge(s) of other doctors (peer review).

- Doctors have an obligation to society to perform that arduous task.

- Doctors, unfortunately, do not have the authority, moral or otherwise, to fulfill that obligation to society.

- Therefore, medical malpractice litigation will remain the treatment of choice for the review of questionable patient care.

Organized Medicine has long accepted that Sophia's Choice. I refuse to accept it. Medical peer review is the only system that can fulfill all of what is necessary to create a true medical profession and a health care system we all deserve. The first thing that must be overcome is the multitudes shouting, "Impossible!" while ignoring the fact that we all stand on the shoulders of those who did the impossible.

Third Recommendation: The Individual Responsibility Peer Review System: Individual Responsibility Peer Review (IRPR). Four letters and a few easy steps, how can doctors be convinced or forced into taking them?

An IRPR system says to every individual doctor,

"Doctor, you take care of the person you see in the mirror each morning, and the IRPR system will take care of the medical malpractice problem."

Questionable patient care is a natural byproduct of the practice of medicine. Why? Because the practice of medicine is one human treating another human using advanced scientific technologies. All humans make human mistakes.

No system of questionable patient care review will eliminate that part of the human equation. So, the next best alternative is to create a system of review that is as fundamentally sound as humanly possible and is fair to both doctor and patient. Any system that does not balance the scales of fair review equally, between both doctor and patient, will lack credibility and professional integrity. An IRPR system, properly organized and justly administered can provide both of those absolute necessities.

The On *Button:* Probably every hospital medical staff in America would say they have either:

- Standing departmental peer review committees.

- A standing hospital medical staff peer review committee.

- A hospital medical staff peer review system.

With medical peer review legislatively made secret, no details of past or present medical staff peer review functions can be discussed. You would think that federal and state legislatures might begin to wonder exactly what benefits to society was obtained by that collective agreement to make medical peer review secret over twenty years ago. It appears that "Don't ask, don't tell!" doesn't only apply to the military. Does Bernie Madoff and the SEC come to mind for anyone here?

Do systems of hospital medical staff peer review exist?
Yes.
Do they function on a regular basis and with a systematic manner?
No!

One of the major reasons for the monumental lapse of using a key ingredient to satisfy a basic professional obligation to society is the lack of an *on* button. Pressing it is equal to initiating the review process. Any hospital medical staff claiming to have an existing medical staff peer review system should be able to describe, in detail, the person or persons that are allowed to initiate activity within that system.

I initiated medical staff peer review activity in the three private hospitals in Madison, Wisconsin, and the University of Wisconsin Hospital and Clinics where I practiced. While each hospital medical staff responded differently, they were all less than professional. During my first experience in requesting medical peer review, as the second surgeon, for that patient's original treatment, which was exceedingly negligent, I was asked by that hospital's medical director, "Are you a troublemaker?"

It is far too easy to rapidly pass over that question that goes right to the heart of the matter and that everyone involved in seeking higher quality health care should be required to answer. Was I, or any other well-intended practitioner, acting as a troublemaker? America's health care system has for far too long been in this quality chasm quandary, precisely because too few people have been asking the hard questions.

A medical peer review system cannot be said to truly exist where no one can identify who is eligible to hit that system's *on* button, or even to hit that button knowing that there will be a price to pay. I paid that price as illustrated in the chapter "Tales from the Dark Side."

Organized Medicine cannot identify a proven medical peer review track record anywhere in America because they will not tolerate practitioners who might initiate that system, and because doctors don't know how to judge other doctors if such a system were to be initiated. Hospital administrations and medical staff leaders go into spasms the rare times they are forced, and that is the only way it can occur, to respond to such a request.

Activators of the IRPR system: The on *button must be accessible to individuals medically qualified or legally justified to do so.*

Legally Justified: Patient, spouse, immediate family member, or legal guardian.

Medically Qualified: Hospital medical staff members and hospital employees having direct patient care responsibilities such as OR, ICU, and ER nurses, etc.

Only a hospital medical staff dedicated to the ethical foundation of their profession and to the community they have chosen to serve can create, establish, and fairly administer an IRPR system.

America has an estimated six thousand or more hospitals, and those hospitals and their medical staffs are like six thousand or more different people, and they all differ in size, make-up, personalities, etc. The IRPR system outlined in this manual can be modified into equally differing sizes and shapes to fit the needs of each hospital medical staff. But fundamental elements of the system must remain the same in every IRPR system of questionable patient care review.

After an IRPR system is firmly established and the medical staff members see a system that can fairly judge questionable patient care, the treating doctors may, at times, activate the system for review of their own patient care. Malpractice litigation denies a doctor the review of their personal track record of patient care, which I believe is the best means of identifying good doctors who will occasionally make common, human mistakes. The competent physician's best friend can be found in a properly functioning IRPR system of peer review.

The poorly qualified physician's worst nightmare can be found in that exact same system.

Medical Staff Peer Review Coordinator: An IRPR system once activated must have a gatekeeper: Staffing this position will vary by hospital size and medical staff make-up. Medical staff designation of such a person may range from the chief of staff or medical director at larger hospitals to possibly even a highly qualified nurse at smaller hospitals.

The key issue is that the peer review coordinator has unquestionable authority and the full support of the hospital administration and medical staff in order to fulfill the obligations of that position. Resistance to proper response by any medical staff member to requests from the peer review coordinator cannot, and must not, be tolerated.

A properly functioning IRPR system can never be created and utilized unless it is clearly understood that every physician on the medical staff, from the chief of staff down to the newest member, may be subject to IRPR review if they are actively treating patients at that hospital. Any deviation from that understanding will render an IRPR system a sham.

Medical Staff Member Subject to Peer Review: After the peer review coordinator has responded to that system's activation and made sufficient inquiry and medical record review to establish a need for full IRPR review, *the medical staff member will be notified that such review will be rapidly undertaken.*

IRPR review is a review of a practitioner's personal patient care track record; therefore, *at least three patient care medical records will be included in the review process.* Should red flags become evident during the initial review process, additional patient care records of similar types of treatment will be added to the review.

One of the most insidious forms of negligent patient care is the use of out-dated, substandard methods of care. An IRPR system of peer review offers Organized Medicine an opportunity to raise the bar of patient care from the legally acceptable medical standard of care presently "set at the lowest possible hurdle" to a far more professional current and acceptable standard of care level. It is in the zone of medical practice located between those two differing standards of care that the unqualified and marginally qualified practitioners will be identified as illustrated previously in What Went Wrong?

The medical staff member to be reviewed will supply for purposes of that review the following:

1. Documentation of personal training and experience necessary for that form of patient care (on an as-needed basis).

2. All out-patient medical records, photos, laboratory reports, x-rays, etc. associated with the treatment of the three similar cases being reviewed, with the understanding that additional cases will be reviewed if indicated.

3. Treatment-specific Informed Consent forms, i.e., a total-hip replacement patient would be given a total-hip replacement Informed Consent form prior to surgery.

4. A signed affidavit of cooperation. Every medical staff member of a hospital having an IRPR system of peer review will be required to have signed an affidavit offering full cooperation when the subject of IRPR review and full participation when requested to serve as a reviewer.

5. A detailed, itemized checklist of the scientific elements of that practitioner's personal standard of care for the specific form of medical care being reviewed. (See Appendix C)

The list of scientific elements for the treatment being reviewed allows doctors of different specialties to fairly peer review other doctors. For instance, a peer review committee made up of an internist, a general surgeon, and an urologist can fairly peer review an orthopedic surgeon. Any person who can master sufficient knowledge of neuro-anatomy and biochemistry to graduate from medical school can follow the steps of a standard of care checklist and compare those to what actually occurred as noted in the patient's medical record.

Treatment-specific standard of care checklists and the multiple, personal track record patient care review are where Organized Medicine can begin to separate the qualified practitioners from the unqualified. Once a properly functioning IRPR system of peer review has been established long enough to demonstrate fair medical peer review is possible, the qualified practitioners should feel a great weight lifted from their mental shoulders. It is like saying, "Doctor, go and practice the kind of medicine you are personally capable of."

Insight: Every practicing physician who has no single engine flight experience should go take at least two flying lesions. The purpose being to experience the difference between the science and the art of flying an airplane. Then they must translate that experience into a much deeper understanding of the difference between the science and art of medicine. Lastly, they must incorporate that new appreciation of the two indispensable characteristics of all medical care into their personal care of every future patient. The airplane checklist provides the scientific elements of flying a particular type airplane from preflight, start engine and take-off, to landing and engine off. (See Appendix D)

Just as two hydrogen molecules and one oxygen molecule make up water, the science and art of every form of medical care make-up each treatment form standard of care. Quality of care experts should either cease to use the airline industry model in their search to cross the quality chasm, or better yet, use the entire spectrum of safety benefits one can gain from the airline industry. Half a loaf is not necessarily better than none in all cases.

The medical standard of care must cease to be

some nebulous, theoretical entity and become a clearly definable medical truth. Standard is defined as a rule used as a basis for judgment. The quality chasm has long existed because the medical standard of care has never fulfilled the promise of that definition.

Peer Review Committee: At least three medical staff members are necessary for this IRPR requirement. At first it may be viewed as a thankless job, but someone has to do it. Once firmly established, it will be an opportunity to establish the practice of medicine as a true profession in the eyes of that local community. *The practice of medicine will take on a new meaning.*

To establish an IRPR system, initially a hospital medical staff will probably be forced to form multiple three-member peer review teams created by lot drawn, or some other reasonable method. Those committees have an equal obligation to both doctor and patient.

Each peer review committee member will take one of the three initial patient care cases and a copy of the practitioner's standard of care checklist, and then do a step-by-step review of that patient's care. The best advice a Peer Review Committee member can receive is, "Let the chips fall where they may." Peer Review Committee members are neither practitioner's protectors nor patients' advocates. They represent *all of the above!*

Time is of the essence.

Patient care review demands a prompt response from all parties involved. Peer Review Committee members who are less than diligent or biased toward doctors must be censored in the strongest manner. The professional integrity of that local medical community rests in their hands.

The three Peer Review Committee members will meet and jointly review each member's findings. Red flags will be noted for sufficient indication that additional patient care medical records should be added to the review process. It is imperative that the treatment-specific patient care track record of every medical staff member being reviewed be of a *current* and *acceptable* nature. Outmoded patient care techniques must be identified and eliminated for the benefit of the local community.

A joint meeting of the Peer Review Committee and the staff member being investigated will be held following sufficient review of multiple patient care records. A list of concerns and questionable patient care items will be presented to them as necessary. Favorable findings of quality patient care will also be noted.

The IRPR system allows a hospital medical staff to differentiate between acceptable patient care with complications and negligent patient care (a major failing medical malpractice litigation can never satisfy). No other system of questionable patient care review judges a practitioner's art of medicine and allows a doctor's patient care track record to demonstrate that doctor's quality of care. Here, too, is where the medical staff can discover those practitioners who may have added new patient care procedures to their personal scope of practice without proper credentialing or qualification.

The medical staff member being reviewed will be asked to review in detail any questionable items regarding:

- Pre-treatment diagnosis and treatment planning.

- Treatment-specific aspects of patient care including elements of surgeries or invasive procedures involved within that treatment.

- Post-treatment aspects of patient care.

- Need for consultations.*

- Complications, actual and/or anticipated as highly possible.

- Subject member's summation of all events that led to the IRPR review process.

- Clarification of differences of opinion between subject member and the committee findings.

- Peer Review Committee reports to the peer review coordinator.

    *Consultations demand specific requirements:

        -All consultations requested from qualified sources who accept the consultation obligation.

-All request for consultations be noted in the patient's medical record with documentation of need for the consultation and medical support sought.

-Acceptance by the consultant to be noted in the patient's medical record.

-Detailed findings by the consultant to be noted in the patient's medical record.

The Patient's Medical Record: There are two very important fundamentals of every patient's medical record that should be understood by those seeking to improve the quality of health care through the review of questionable patient care. First, the combination of the patient and their medical record provides the "art" of an individual practitioner's art of medicine. Second, the patient medical record is one of the most abused aspects of the practice of medicine anywhere in America today. *It would take someone only minutes in any hospital medical record department to find numerous examples of negligent documentation of specific patient care. Furthermore, AMA, JC, all state hospital associations, and particularly all hospital medical record department staff know that to be true, and that outrage has been passively accepted.*

The unwritten rule regarding patient's medical records is: if it's not written it didn't occur. Negligent documentation is the first shortcoming found in many, if not most, patient medical records. Unadulterated arrogance in the form of illegible orders and progress notes scrawled across the page exudes contempt and is also common in medical records.

If you want to see the perfidy of health care in America, take a close look at numerous patient medical records shortly after a hospital has received a clean bill of health from the Joint Commission. They talk of having accountability when meaningful accountability is not evident. Hospitals advertise cardio-vascular surgery, orthopedic surgery, ob-gyn surgery and others "to a higher standard."

If they know the present treatment is to a "higher standard," then they must know the previous standard. Yet the AMA defines malpractice as treatment beneath a standard of care "set by the law." If one were ever allowed to closely review fifty patient medical records of any specialty claiming patient care to a higher standard, I believe those ads would disappear.

Accountability, standards, peer review, and other words used to describe current medical care in America have no fundamental support in fact. The practice of medicine is the least regulated economic activity in America, and Organized Medicine provides the least amount of factual accountability.

This much too brief outline of an IRPR system of medical peer review will unintentionally mislead some into assuming it to be too simplistic for the task it is meant to accomplish. The deficiency lies in the form of presentation. The most comprehensive way to be introduced to the IRPR system would be by using a live audience of open-mined people seeking ways to improve the existing health care system.

The IRPR system of medical peer review can be expanded far beyond current imagination and only a live audience presentation with audience participation can first demonstrate that system's full potential.

Medical malpractice litigation is and has been the primary system utilized by Organized Medicine for the review of questionable patient care. I have actively participated in the medical malpractice litigation system a sufficient number of times to appreciate how monumentally flawed that system is and has always been. I believe doctors and patients deserve a far better system of patient care review.

Civil court litigation is conducted under the restraints of "rules of evidence" and other legal hindrances to rational review. Frequently, obvious questions cannot be asked or answers given unless a legal foundation for that line of questions has been established. Civil court legal limitations can easily befuddle all listeners except the judge and attorneys present. It is probably impossible to fairly judge the diverse essentials of questionable patient care through civil court litigation, yet lay jurors are asked to do just that all too often.

There are no rules of evidence in an IRPR system of medical peer review. Doctors can talk freely, using professional terms. Straightforward questions should be asked, and straightforward answers should ensue.

Society must be protected from doctors who cannot or will not demonstrate the ability to rationally present what they did to a patient, how they did it, and why they did it as they did. Medical peer review is the only cure for the medical malpractice crisis, and no, attorneys are not the primary cause of that crisis, regardless of what the AMA says.

My experience in medical malpractice litigation and medical peer review allows me to guarantee that an IRPR system, properly utilized, can develop far beyond anyone's imagination in creating a system of peer review fair to both doctor and patient. Therefore, consider this contrast in reasoning:

- Medical malpractice litigation is a system despised by doctors and patients.

- IRPR is a system that can restore doctors to being in charge of their profession and would be the "good doctors" best friend.

Yet every time I have attempted to speak with doctors about the IRPR system of medical peer review I have been met with instant, strong, negative exceptions as to why such a system is "impossible." Doctors practicing medicine in the litigious climate *they created* cannot comprehend a system of doctors fairly judging other doctors. It's like I am talking about science fiction in such discussions. That is why a live presentation would allow them to be walked through the entire process prior to their making a judgment regarding its feasibility.

The Big Lie!

A survey of over 1,600 doctors taken late last year revealed:

- 46% of doctors admitted to not reporting a serious medical error they had witnessed.

- 45% admitted to not reporting a physician whom they knew to be impaired or incompetent.

Dr. David Blumenthal, Director of the Institute for Health Policy at Massachusetts General Hospital, a professor at Harvard Medical School and an IOM member said about the results of his survey that:

- He was not shocked by physicians' failure to report these errors.

- The result did not surprise him because reporting a colleague is "very awkward" and can "open the doors to legal complications."

- It would be helpful to have *legal training* at every level of medical education.

Compare the results of that survey to the AMA Code of Medical Ethics:

A physician shall deal honestly with patients and colleagues and strive to expose those physicians deficient in character or competence or who engage in fraud or deception.

I do *not* consider Dr. Blumenthal to be a liar!

Why not? Practically everyone currently involved in health care accept The Big Lie as the Gospel of Medical Peer Review proclaimed by HCQIA–1986 when almighty Congress deemed medical peer review *secret*. The results of that nonsensical decision have been a complete disaster!

True medical peer review does *not* exist in America.

The results of Dr. Blumenthal's "survey" reminds me of what is taking place in the Gulf of Aden where ship captains are surrendering to Somali pirates, most of whom may be unable to read or write. It seems to me that Dr. Blumenthal's medical staff has waved a white flag of surrender to any attorney who might threaten them with "legal consequences." Does today's medical profession have no shame? A closer examination of the real worlds of medical peer review and malpractice litigation should improve the perspective of each.

A recent article in the local newspaper regarding a patient's successful medical malpractice lawsuit against doctors of a local, nationally recognized orthopedic surgery clinic can offer some insight into the medical peer review vs. medical malpractice litigation debate.

The Greenville News, November 4, 2009: Union, SC, man wins suit over surgery: A fuel delivery truck driver injured his shoulder in late 2003 and underwent three unsuccessful surgeries in 2004. The second and third surgeries were done by a principle partner of that prestigious surgery clinic and an assisting surgeon in training. The third unsuccessful surgery resulted in extensive damage to a major nerve in the surgical area that has resulted in severe pain and lost of muscle tone to his right arm.

Testimony supported the fact that the patient had signed an informed consent indicating that the nationally recognized surgeon would be performing that third surgery, when in fact the fellow surgeon in training performed the surgery and dictated in his operative notes that the nerve in question was visualized during surgery. If properly performed, that nerve should not have been seen. The resultant jury award to the patient and another to his wife was for over 1 million dollars.

This sad story could easily be viewed as just one more harmful medical event unless one chooses to seek deeper insight into medical peer review and medical malpractice litigation. The last two unsuccessful surgeries were apparently performed at a freestanding surgery clinic adjacent to one of the hospitals in the Greenville-Spartanburg SC area and were performed in 2004. In another newspaper's article regarding 'Medical secrets' Greenville and Spartanburg area hospital officials are quoted as saying they use peer review extensively. In that same article the

South Carolina Medical Association chief executive officer is quoted as saying, "No one would disclose anything if it was open (peer review) and such reviews are a logical, scientific investigation of everything that happened to an injured or deceased patient–have been around for decades but are underutilized. A trial lawyer would love to know what happens during these peer review cases."

A Greenville Hospital System vice president is quoted in a third article "Sorry Works" as saying their system averages about seventeen lawsuits a year. So let's go back and connect some dots. That patient with the successful lawsuit in 2009 had received three unsuccessful surgeries in 2004. Also, Greenville and Spartanburg area hospital officials say that they use peer review extensively, but since medical peer review was made secret by Congress, followed by all 50 states, because the medical profession told Congress that medical peer review could only function under a cloak of secrecy no one really knows if or when medical peer review becomes more fact than myth.

That patient who had received three unsuccessful surgeries in 2004 is forced to presume that those questionable treatment outcomes did receive "scientific investigation," but since medical peer review was made secret he and his wife were forced to wait for five years, while the wheels of the medical malpractice litigation system turned, all that time being left with a useless right arm.

There was no indication that this patient's lawsuit was labeled one of the medical profession's favorite canards, a "frivolous lawsuit." The question doctors should be asked is, when do reasonable questions regarding questionable patient care become frivolous, and who determines that change in classification from reasonable to frivolous? Frivolous lawsuits exist because our medical profession has never created a system whereby reasonable questions regarding questionable patient care can receive meaningful answers from within their profession, rapidly and at the site of patient care. Attorneys, courts, and juries create the frivolous nature of questionable patient care, not the patients.

In the article "Medical secrets," it was noted, "Of the medical examiner board's eighty-six disciplinary actions made public in the past two years, three dealt with standard of care, according to a Community Journals review." South Carolina can be justifiably proud of one fact: no other state medical examining board could provide a more effective track record regarding the review of questionable patient care. Thus society has always been left with the myth of medical peer review and the fact of sue or forget it."

Remember that twenty-seven-year-old wife and mother who expected to receive minor knee surgery under local anesthesia and instead was rendered clinically dead within minutes? On the third anniversary of her "needless" death a lay jury declared, "No negligence!" But where might one find any evidence of "scientific investigation" regarding that tragic event? Certainly not from the ones who should be the best judges of questionable patient care—other doctors. Caveat emptor, let the buyer beware! Medical malpractice tort reform, to be covered in more detail later, guarantees the public that medical malpractice litigation will continue to be the system of choice should you or a loved one become the victim of a "never event."

Every health care organization, including Organized Medicine, has meekly abdicated their responsibility for some degree of regulation of the practice of medicine to attorneys, courts, and juries. This passive surrender to the threat of legal action is based upon a monumental distortion of *fact!*

If this distortion was truly fact, anarchy should reign throughout our nation, because all regulatory efforts should like-wise be ruled invalid. If this rational is to be accepted, than no governmental agency has the power to regulate airline pilots, truck drivers, etc.

The underlying reason why the practice of medicine is held captive by the threat of litigation is because there has never been a proper regulatory system for the practice of medicine created at any level of government and anywhere in the nation. State legislatures, and state legislatures alone, are the primary cause of every medical malpractice crisis. There lies the responsibility for the regulation of the practice of medicine and of hospital medical staffs and now of freestanding surgery clinics.

Focus for a moment on one aspect of the ACOG peer review article mentioned earlier. Disruptive practitioners—thirty-eight out of one hundred site visits. The impact on all of the other practitioners in that department and all of the nursing and ancillary staff goes far beyond merely a one-line statistic in a medical journal article. Patients, the most important ingredient in the medical equation, wasn't even mentioned in that article, but it is the patients who are most impacted by such unethical and unprofessional, but tolerated physician behavior.

Everyone involved who is forced to constantly deal with even one disruptive practitioner within his or her department is adversely affected. Yet Dr. Blumenthal, and seemingly everyone else, has passively accepted the "fact" that medical peer review for the control and regulation of practitioner staff behavior is a captive of "potential retaliatory litigation." The inmates truly have taken control of the asylum.

I offer the following considerations for social response to those who consider a viable IRPR system to be impossible:

- *Walk away from those who can tell you what they are against but cannot tell you what they are for.*

- *Run away from those who tell you they can recognize the impossible.*

Several decades ago every *expert* in the world, but one, said, "It is impossible to replace natural teeth with metal post replacements!" Professor Branemark of Sweden said, "I think I can do that." The world now enjoys the benefits of dental implants.

We stand on the shoulders of those who refused to recognize "the impossible," and where would we be today without such people?

Test Question: IRPR system of medical peer review would ask doctors who had provided questionable patient care three questions:

1. Do you have the training, experience, and medical staff credentials that would allow you to provide this type patient care?

2. Will you cooperate freely and completely with a review of your patient care?

3. Do you appreciate the benefit of having your patient care performance be based upon your past track record of the specific form of patient care in question?

Which form of questionable patent care review would a reader prefer to be used at the hospital nearest them?

*   IOM—AHRQ—NQF national standards

*   Joint Commission standards

*   DNV—ISO 9001 standards

*   Common Good special malpractice courts

- Baldrige national quality standards

- IRPR

- Any other type review system unlisted

Only an IRPR system of peer review identifies the specific points of *authority* and *responsibility* and more importantly, it provides a means for *rapid accountability* by members of that hospital's medical staff (doctors judging other doctors) and at the site of the questionable patient care.

The anticipated time line is another very positive potential attribute:

- Phase one: IRPR peer review–6 months or less.

- Phase two: Mediation* and I'm Sorry!–6 months or less.

- Phase three: Malpractice litigation–only if necessary and only after one year.

Compare that scenario to the current, protracted malpractice litigation, medical malpractice tort reform process presently being offered the public as a "social benefit." *Mediation has never become a highly effective tool in questionable patient care review because it can best function *after* a sound judgment regarding that care has been made. IRPR will finally make mediation a vital component of questionable patient care review.

Also let me describe what should be obvious, but

obviously isn't, to those who say they are using the airline industry as a model for greater patient safety. When one of the miraculously few commercial airline crashes occurs in America one process rapidly begins and a second set of process(es) may begin:

- FAA immediately begins a thorough investigation as that system's regulatory agency.

- Civil litigation for victims and/or survivors may be initiated whether with justifiable cause or not.

The regulatory agency review is entirely separate and independent of the litigation process, as it should be. Those health care experts seeking to use the airline industry as a model for improved quality of health care and greater patient safety must use all aspects of that industry. There is no reason why the threat of civil litigation should be allowed to stifle the desperately needed use of medical peer review from becoming the best regulatory tool in the review of questionable patient care.

Dr. Lucian Leape has been a leading advocate of the "*nonpunitive* systems approach" to the prevention of medical errors. Such thinking begs the question, is the FAA being "punitive" when in the course of aircraft accident review they determine that accident was due to pilot error? Therefore is it punitive for doctors to judge the questionable patient care provided by other doctors?

Patient Safety Activists across the nation work

tirelessly to obtain better patient safety regulation through state legislative enactments while the health care cottage industry cabal of IOM, AHRQ, NQF, NPSF, IHI and others continue to seek health care improvement through national standards, systems errors and nonpunitive responses. Does no one see the huge disconnect between the thrust of those efforts?

All health care is local. A system of questionable patient care review must be established by the state, but to be effective, it must function at a site closest to the patient care in question and as rapidly as possible. The hospital medical staff is the most ideal place for effective questionable patient care review, and like the Harvard Medical School Department of Anesthesia minimum standards, IRPR can be utilized in every hospital in America. It seems foolish to continue to ignore how over 20 years ago seven minimum safety standard "lines in the sand" created such a rapid and positive patient safety impact suitable for use in every hospital in the nation while the health care patient safety cottage industry continues to seek to utilize "national standards."

Can anyone save patients from the experts?

Perspective: Department of Health and Human Services (DHHS) Secretary Kathleen Sebelius (KS) and the two past DHHS secretaries Tommy Thompson (WI) and Michael Leavitt (NV) are all past governors of states having one or more medical schools and each of those individuals are touted to have great health care expertise. In fact, the DHHS is reported to be "the United States government's principal agency for protecting the health of all Americans." Yet none of them can show evidence of awareness that since states license most doctors to practice medicine those same states are required to regulate every aspect of medical practice within their state.

America is literally drowning in health care expertise at every level of our health care "system" while our health care "system" is drowning in disorganized chaos. One reason is that health care "experts" are not being forced to accept and answer the many hard questions concerning our current health care system and the changes being offered.

Readers should stop and consider a very obvious, but unacknowledged fact; when Brennan, Leape, and others began their monumental study in New York state hospitals in 1986 it was the state, and not the federal government, that permitted authorization and access for that study that identified the now famous estimate of 98,000 needless hospital deaths annually in 1990.

Examine a partial list:

Eleven congressional committees have primary jurisdiction over legislation pertinent to hospitals and other health care institutions.

DHHS has 12 divisions and responsibility for oversight of the Joint Commission.

PSRO—PRO—QIO.

Institute of Medicine

National Quality Forum (created by the Clinton Administration).

40 Schools of Public Health and 8 Associate Schools of Public Health.

Non-governmental health care agencies:

National Patient Safety Foundation and the Lucian Leape Institute.

Dr. Donald Berwick's Institute for Healthcare Improvement.

Robert Wood Johnston and Duke Foundations and others.

State health care agencies

The list could go on and on and the first question that should be asked is, "What's missing?" The entire package of JC hospital certification, IOM recommendations, AHRQ-NQF 30 Points, national standards, evidence-based medicine, practitioner data bank, PSRO-PRO-QIO, etc. is that they all just hang out there in empty space. Why? They all fail to fulfill their intended purpose(s) because they all lack an organizational structure containing clearly evident points of authority, responsibility and accountability that would allow each to function properly at the site of patient care in every hospital and surgery center. That AMA Vice President, Dr. Audiey Kao summed it up perfectly in his comments on finding the art of medicine. Without an identifiable organizational structure for the entire health care system that permits proper function at the local site of patient care it all becomes *idealistic rhetoric!*

No one has been seeking to describe the organizational structure of the system that affects every citizen and no one has recognized the simple fact that if states license doctors then states are responsible to regulate their practice and therefore each state is responsible to create a regulatory mechanism that functions and is identifiable. Every state must be forced to find their "black box" containing their medical practice regulatory mechanism.

A seemingly endless supply of health care experts talk confidently about making our health care system better and improving the quality and safety of patient care while never speaking about each state's responsibility to contribute to those efforts. Chaos will continue to reign in our health care system until health care decision makers are forced to take and answer the hard questions of exactly where are we now and how did we get here?

"What is the cost of your system of medical peer review?" A man with great state legislative experience very recently asked me that thought-provoking question and it resulted in several vastly different answers.

Has anyone ever asked, "What is the cost to regulate automobile drivers, traffic violations and DUI?" If the state licenses any endeavor is that state automatically responsible to regulate the corresponding individual activity?

Also, sources have been saying lately that billions of dollars would be saved over a ten-year period if medical malpractice tort reform was enacted. None of the states identified by the AMA to have "enjoyed" for years highly acceptable MMTR can demonstrate evidence of even miniscule savings due to that false promise and therefore that specious claim should demand hard evidence prior to acceptance.

IRPR will save lives! Look what the Harvard Department of Anesthesia accomplished in one year using seven minimum standards. How does one value saved lives? If IRPR provided half as much greater patient safety the health care cost savings would be staggering. Plus IRPR would rapidly trump the need for Defensive Medicine.

The nation cannot afford not to fully evaluate the IRPR system of medical peer review.

The true test will be to evaluate a complete IRPR system.

If you want to cross the quality chasm, you must create a system of medical regulation through peer review that guides each doctor into:

•   Recognizing the medical scope of their personal ability regarding patient care.

- Recognizing the consequences if they exceed their personal patient care limitations.

If good doctors, the majority, are promised that they will be judged for human mistakes on their personal track record of patient care, a new day in America's health care system will dawn. Unfortunately, all evidence to date indicates that doctors will have to be forced, while kicking and screaming, to make medical peer review the instrument of choice in the review of questionable patient care.

OTHER OFFERINGS

Medical malpractice tort reform and special medical malpractice courts have been used in various forms for decades because of the promise(s) each system has been guaranteed to deliver for greater patient safety. Strangely, no one appears to connect the dots of patient safety reality while touting the potential benefits of those systems.

The staggering number (98,000) of needless hospital deaths annually remains unchanged, while improved patient safety efforts have been surrounded by both medical malpractice tort reform and failed attempts at using special medical malpractice courts.

Current efforts by many well-intentioned individuals to push for more and stronger doses of these two "cures for what ails" the quest for quality health care compels consideration of each.

Medical Malpractice Tort Reform

Truths—Lies—Distortions

Medical Malpractice Tort Reform (MMTR)—a health care conundrum. MMTR has been a major component of health care regulation in various forms and various parts of the nation for over three decades, and currently there is a hue and cry that more and greater types of reform are urgently needed to further protect doctors from the constant threat of malpractice litigation. Thousands, if not millions, of congressional and state legislative hours have been spent dealing with MMTR, and people continue to get lost in creating legal ways to protect doctors from malpractice litigation while treating the other half of the medical care equation, the patient, like an illegitimate child at a family reunion.

The first catastrophic medical malpractice crisis swept the nation in the mid '70s, even though the underlying cause of that crisis had been a fact of medical life for over a hundred years, and three decades later, we still don't get it. Note: A joint AMA/AHA committee predicted the coming medical malpractice crisis about fifteen years before it occurred (JAMA 1958) and Organized Medicine did nothing to prevent it. Why? Our medical profession has never had the capability to deal properly with questionable patient care and therefore could only standby and allow that tragedy to occur as though it was a natural, rather than a man-made disaster.

Medical malpractice, in its basic form, involves one doctor and one patient. MMTR aficionados stare at the doctor part so long they loose sight of the patient. A comprehensive understanding of MMTR, its potential benefits and shortcomings, is necessary to better determine that system's true value in helping to better regulate medical patient care and contribute to health care cost control.

Questionable patient care is a constant reality of health care, because doctors are only human, all humans make mistakes, and the review of questionable patient care is necessary to initiate the process that makes MMTR an end-point consideration. Therefore any in-depth consideration of MMTR should begin with the initial causation.

The need for questionable patient care review has been well established. Patient safety experts estimated that 98,000 needless hospital deaths were occurring annually twenty years ago. Institute of Medicine (IOM) To Err Is Human validated that tragic estimate of annual needless hospital deaths ten years later and promised to reduce that carnage by 50 percent in five years. All current estimates of needless hospital deaths regrettably demonstrate no discernable reduction in spite of great effort by hundreds of highly dedicated and immensely qualified people.

Needless hospital deaths represent only the "tip of the iceberg" regarding questionable patient care, because there are many times more non-fatal incidents of unacceptable medical treatment that should receive thorough review and for the most part do not. Therefore, the need is beyond great, it is long standing, and there is no evidence of the slightest degree of improvement, and the rising cost of health care must take second consideration to the human tragedy this social dilemma represents.

To best understand the dynamics of questionable patient care review, each reader should imagine that they or a loved one has been the recipient of such care and has been denied reasonable explanation and redress for the resultant unacceptable medical out-come.

Once the reality of questionable patient care becomes personal, one is left with seeking to determine what options are available for regulatory relief.

Three systems with the potential to review questionable patient care:

State medical examining boards. Every state's medical examining board's past experience with addressing individual incidents of questionable patient care will be discovered to be all but nonexistent in that regard. Historically, state medical examining boards have proved to be colossally inadequate for that task. Therefore, realistically, a medically harmed person's options for regulatory relief are actually limited to two.

Medical peer review. Every one of our nation's six thousand hospitals would proudly claim the existence of one or more forms of medical peer review within the organizational structure of their medical staff. Few hospitals, if any, however, could provide evidence of comprehensive medical peer review regarding specific incidents of questionable patient care, and none would have to since Congress, closely followed by every state, made medical peer review secret with HCQIA-1986.

Therefore, a person seeking regulatory relief has had their second option shrouded in legislated secrecy because the Medical Profession of America promised Congress that medical peer review could never "function as it should without that veil of secrecy," and they got it. Medical peer review has all of the substance of fog, and thus, persons arguably harmed by questionable patient care have, in all reality, been left with primarily a single option of "sue or forget it."

Medical malpractice litigation (MML):

- MML has always been overwhelmingly the primary system for the review of questionable patient care throughout the history of health care in America, hence the pejorative "sue or forget it."

- AMA has long acknowledged their obligation to society to self-regulate their members regarding questionable patient care and openly proclaimed the obvious, that doctors are the best judge(s) of other doctors (or should be).

- AMA acknowledgement of that obligation has unfortunately never been translated into reality.

- Once an attorney becomes involved in a specific incident of questionable patient care review the medical profession has lost all control of that process.

- MML requires both a physically and psychologically impaired patient or loved one(s) to add to their current trauma the mantel of accuser, plus the enormous financial and psychological burdens of protracted litigation.

- Medical malpractice, the judgment, cannot exist without expert witness testimony, except in the very rare cases of res ipsa loquitur (the thing speaks for itself), such as when a doctor amputates the wrong leg.

- AMA, using every means possible, has severely marginalized the very existence of potential expert witnesses for the plaintiff (patient).

- These are just some of the many considerations necessary prior to initiating MML and to see that demeaning process through to its end, all the time knowing that doctors rarely loose MML cases. The odds are enormously unfavorable to the litigant patient.

Medical malpractice tort reform (MMTR) is:

- The legislatively orchestrated transfer of the legal right and benefits of one class of people (patients) to the additional legal benefit of another class of people (doctors).

- Acts as a restrictor plate or governor in the form of an additional deterrent to even consider seeking regulatory redress through the MML process.

- Most importantly, like flood insurance, MMTR provides *zero* benefit for correcting the root cause of the problem, questionable patient care, and equally important, no one can provide evidence that MMTR does now, ever has, or can in the future.

AMA efforts seeking federal MMTR included the following statements:

- *Will Your Doctor Be There? (Brochure 2003):* "The primary cause of America's medical liability crisis is overzealous personal injury attorneys who put their pocketbooks before patients." Question: How, When, and Where did an attorney cause any patient's questionable medical care problem? That statement is just one of the lies perpetrated on the American public by the AMA and others and never questioned.

- *Medical Liability Reform—NOW! June 14, 2004:* California Medical Injury Compensation Reform

Act of 1975 (MICRA-75) was considered in 2004 to be the "Gold Standard for MMTR" by the AMA. Such glowing consideration should justify a detailed answer to the following question: "Have the citizens of California enjoyed significantly greater protection from negligent medical care over the past three decades than the citizens of states who have not enjoyed all of the benefits that come from MMTR similar to that found in MICRA-75?" The answer is a resounding *no!* California has continued to contribute more than its fair share to the 98,000 needless hospital deaths annually plus the even larger number of non-fatal medically created carnage.

- If one were ever to ask, "How can the benefit from MMTR to society be measured?" the response would be silence because it can't be measured.

- *MMTR is like buying oceanfront property in Arizona. There is a new one born every day.*

WHO dubiously ranks American health care thirty-seventh in the world behind the likes of Oman, Cyprus, and Chile when the fact is that American health care provides more highly acceptable health care on a daily basis than all of the rest of the world combined. Unfortunately, American health care also provides far more questionable patient care than should be tolerated but has been for far too long.

Questionable patient care *must* become the target

of all discussions regarding the quality of health care, and a system of review fair to both doctor and patient must become the goal of every future discussion.

First, one must acknowledge that state medical examining boards can never fulfill the task of reviewing questionable patient care. That determination leaves two alternatives—medical malpractice litigation (attorneys, courts and juries) and medical peer review.

Questionable patient care occurs in a hospital or doctor's office and a few of the causes of those incidents are turf wars, out-dated forms of treatment, and the ever-present few doctors who are not qualified to retain a license to practice medicine.

Malpractice litigation has *no* ability to judge the difference between a good doctor with a proven track record of acceptable patient care and the worst practitioner in the state. Yet tort reform has long been offered as the cure for what ails the medical profession.

Since doctors are, or should be, the best judge(s) of other doctors, and medical peer review is the only system whereby doctors control the process, the best choice should seemingly be an easy one.

Two fundamental questions can assist in the process of choosing the best system:

- What is the medical profession's obligation to society regarding questionable patient care?

- What is each state legislature's responsibility to

regulate the private practice of medicine, hospital medical staffs, and now freestanding surgery centers?

Medical malpractice tort reform is as beneficial as placing an elaborate bandage on a tumor. So how can anyone think that regulating the monetary judgments determined in a civil court can directly impact the 98,000 needless hospital deaths, in addition to the countless additional non-lethal medical mishaps?

AMA, in 2003, proclaimed that California, Colorado, Indiana, Louisiana, Michigan, and New Mexico had strong MMTR legislation in place. Indisputable proof of the highly effective results obtained in those states must be clearly evident prior to further pursuit of this legalistic nightmare. After over thirty years, such evidence is either readily available or it is not, and the American public should finally be free of being offered a false promise. The fact that the disastrous figure of 98,000 needless hospital deaths annually remains statistically unchanged after twenty years of awareness and concerted effort by so many *should* indicate the fundamental inefficiency of MMTR.

But if all of the above does not put a stake into the heart of the concerted effort for MMTR, then this last consideration should remove all doubt as to the real value of that empty promise. Physicians Insurers Association of America estimates that of all medical malpractice claims filed, only 5 percent go to trial, and doctors win 80 percent of those cases. A mere

0.9 percent end in a jury verdict for the plaintiff. So MMTR only functions if a plaintiff (patient) wins their malpractice suit against a doctor and that occurs less than 1 percent of the very cases that ever see the inside of a court room. Yes, people, MMTR is the "great hope" to cut the cost of health care and achieve greater patient safety.

The pursuit of containing the cost of health care has resulted in the harmed patient becoming an afterthought. Questionable patient care must become the precise target, and a system of questionable patient care review, reasonably fair to both doctor and patient, must become the goal.

Medical malpractice tort reform can never fulfill that desirable need.

Special Medical Malpractice Courts

Four Decades of Hollow Promises

Special Medical Malpractice Courts (SMMC)—great expectations with miniscule reward. The allure of SMMC continues to attract visceral promotion in spite of possessing few redeeming attributes. Civil courts have never (and can never) adjudicated questionable patient care properly, yet the desire to create a medical malpractice caricature of that inadequate system has a cat-like ability of multiple lives.

Historical perspective:

Wisconsin State Legislature provides one example

of the wide range of responses to the first wave of the medical malpractice crisis that struck the medical profession in the mid '70s and continues unabated. Keep in mind that the AMA knew this crisis was coming about fifteen years before it happened and did *nothing* to sound the alarm.

A Medical Malpractice Patient Compensation Panel system was established to free the civil court system of dealing with such matters and expedite the entire process of medical malpractice litigation. A two-tier system afforded patients who sued for less than $10,000 to come before a three-person panel comprised of one attorney, one doctor and one lay person. Suits exceeding $10,000 (and most did) appeared before a five-person panel of one attorney, two doctors and two lay people.

This system included all of the usual civil litigation characteristics such as depositions, discovery, expert witnesses, etc. Either party, doctor or patient, were free to dispute the panel verdict later in civil court if sufficiently dissatisfied with the finding, and if one episode of legalistic torture wasn't enough.

The true value of Wisconsin's experience with special medical malpractice courts back then was properly expressed when the Wisconsin legislature miraculously dissolved their creation after ten years or less. Having participated in more than one of those experiments in quasi-justice, I can testify that their demise was long overdue. The Wisconsin Medical

Malpractice Patient Compensation Panel system's greatest achievement was to create another source of attorney income, and since most state legislatures are predominantly made up of attorneys, that fact should not come as a surprise.

But bad ideas have a habit of being reborn in altered configurations.

AMA/Specialty Society Medical Liability Project (Medical Liability Project): The MLP was taking form in 1986, about the time the Wisconsin special malpractice courts were becoming an after-thought. AMA announced publicly in January 1988, how the adjudication of malpractice claims by an administrative agency, either a modified state medical licensing board or a brand-new state agency could rescue the public from this social curse.

The book, Medical Malpractice Solutions: Systems and Proposals for Injury Compensation edited by Martin M. Haley, M.D., J.D. and others and published in 1989, devoted Chapter 10 to the AMA's The Model Medical Liability and Patient Protection Act: A Fault-Based Administrative System For Resolving Medical Liability Claims. The AMA's desire was to convince at least two state legislatures to create an opportunity to test this new concept of how to provide "fair and efficient resolution" for medical liability disputes. One facet of that system was to have *claims reviewers* from the Medical Board quickly evaluate claims and dismiss those without merit. Two states,

Utah and Vermont were said to be seriously evaluating the possible implementation of this system by their medical societies.

Two facts summarize the value of this venture into how to improve the systems then being used for the review of questionable patient care. AMA/Specialty Society Medical Liability Project disappeared in the mid '90s without the fanfare used to herald its creation, and none of the Medical Malpractice Solutions offered in that book have seemingly proved to be up to the task of stemming the tide of 98,000 needless hospital deaths estimated simultaneously with its publication. The stark reality of the health care quality chasm and those medical malpractice solutions were like two ships passing in the night.

But bad ideas have a habit of being reborn in altered configurations.

Common Good is the latest creation in the quest for fairness and efficiency in the review of questionable patient care. Newt Gingrich and Attorney Phillip Howard, supported by over eighty academic, political, medical, and legal leaders and consumer advocates orchestrated this attempt to prove that "special health courts" would be the cure for our nation's medical malpractice dilemma in 2002.

These special courts are to have full-time judges, dedicated solely to addressing health care cases, panels of neutral experts in each area of medicine, and will offer speedy proceedings, lower costs, and liberalized recovery for injured patients. If all of that appears to be too good to be true, then perhaps it is. Common Good may have had Bernie Madoff writing their promotional literature, because after seven years, Common Good's special courts remain far more theory than fact, and for good reason.

South Carolina is nationally ranked fortieth in size and twenty-seventh in population. It has sixty-five hospitals, sixty-eight surgery centers, and three major population centers. Common Good, late in 2008, was unable to estimate how many special courts a state similar to South Carolina would require, and they were unable to identify any persons qualified to fill the positions of full time judges or neutral experts in each area of medicine.

Common Good's concept of special medical malpractice courts is a pipe dream sold to the likes of Robert Wood Johnson Foundation and countless others. If full-time judges and neutral experts weren't fantasizing enough, the thought that such a system, if ever implemented, could be cost-effective, is pure lunacy.

Summary: Logic, seemingly a rarity in most health care considerations throughout the history of health care in America, should require a detailed comparison between the disastrous reality of patient safety and how that unacceptable fact may have benefited in the slightest from over three decades of exposure to the AMA's Gold Standard of MMTR, California's

MICRA-75. Fool me once, shame on you. Fool me for over three decades, and shame on everyone involved.

The same need for logic exists with the consideration for special malpractice courts. Begin with: fifty states, over six thousand hospitals, and twice as many surgery centers, an estimated 800,000 or more doctors, and then ask how many courts, how many neutral experts, how many judges, how long to set this system in a functional state, and at what cost? Betting that the Detroit Lions will win the next NFL Super Bowl would be a safer bet than betting that special medical malpractice courts will make a major improvement in patient safety in the next twenty years.

How long must patient safety wait?

Recent Additions to the Health Care Mix

Baldrige National Quality Program: Health care cottage industry has a closely related, relatively new ally in their drive to set national quality standards. Those allies are the Baldrige National Quality Program, National Institute of Standards, and Technology (NIST), an agency of the U.S. Department of Commerce and American Society for Quality (ASQ).

My state has established the South Carolina Quality Forum that awards various levels of the S.C. Governor's Quality award based upon the Baldrige National

Quality criteria. One of Greenville, S.C., two hospital systems received the SC Governor's Quality award for achieving quality standards in late 2008. People all over the state literally gushed over the reported quality performance standards achieved by each of the organizations honored by the SC Quality Forum.

How can anyone draw concern from such highly celebrated honorary attainments? Patient Safety Activists should consider my deep concern for *all* national quality standard-setting efforts, regardless of the source. Baldrige National Quality Program efforts are exceedingly positive endeavors and have contributed greatly to commerce and industry. The concern comes when the focus on national standards replaces the long-sought-for-but-never-achieved goal of creating quality patient care at the individual doctor-patient interface.

Our health care system is literally awash in national standards of varying types promulgated by IOM, AHRQ, NQF, JC, and many others long before the new kid on the block, Baldrige. Real quality health care can *never* be achieved until a system of questionable patient care review is established at every hospital medical staff that permits doctors to fairly judge other doctors. There is *no* suggestion contained here to diminish the value of the Baldrige National Quality Program or similar efforts. There is a clear declaration that national standards alone can *never* achieve the desperately needed goal of quality patient care at the site of delivery.

If one reads the Baldrige National Quality Program Health Care Criteria for Performance Excellence perhaps that person will wonder, as I do, exactly how does that program differ from and provide to hospital administrations quality standard guidelines that the Joint Commission has not been seeking over the last forty plus years? Has the Baldrige program created quality standards that far surpass those of the long-standing JC standards that have supposedly been met on a regular basis?

Far more importantly, can the health care cottage industry show tangible proof that all of their past efforts for establishing national standards have been as beneficial at "the point of treatment delivery" in hospitals across the nation, as the patient safety benefits demonstrated by the Harvard Medical School Department of Anesthesia over 20 years ago? I don't think so.

Recent cottage industry quotes include, "errors are caused by faulty systems, processes and conditions" and are best dealt with by "creating non-punitive environments." and "We cannot expect health care organizations to make patient safety a local priority if we do not make patient safety a national priority." I strongly suggest that this latter reasoning has put the cart before the horse. National quality health care will remain more a hope than a reality until a local system of patient care quality control becomes fully functional and is then reproduced throughout the national health care system.

National cottage industry leaders extol the airline industry as an example of successfully using a "system's errors" approach to obtain higher quality performance.

That would be an acceptable comparison except for one glaring omission. Airline pilots face a rigorous system of individual performance testing on a regular basis that demands each pilot demonstrate *current* and *acceptable* capability. Quality of medicine would dramatically improve if Organized Medicine would incorporate *all* of the positive attributes of the airline industry involving practitioner competency.

National quality standards and their accompanying awards make for great press releases as long as no one compares them to the fact that the IOM promised ten years ago to reduce the rate of needless hospital deaths by 50 percent in five years, and ten years later, that national shame remains unchanged. During the past ten years or more, the cottage industry has become more and more enamored with national standards of care, and there is *no* evidence that society has been a beneficiary. How many needless hospital deaths will it take to force those who control the health care quality debate to consider other ways to reach that long-sought goal?

The second recent addition to the health care mix

comes in the form of competition for the JC in Medicare certification of hospitals by DNV Healthcare, a division of the Norwegian conglomerate, Det Norske Veritas.

DNV Healthcare: "DNV's innovative NIAHO accreditation program passed the rigorous evaluation process, and the US Centers for Medicare and Medicaid Services (CMS) announced its approval for DNV to become a new hospital accreditation organization in September 2008. Thus, DNV became the first new hospital accreditation organization in more than 40 years."

The new hospital accreditation program encourages innovation within individual hospitals while helping them take advantage of system-wide best practices. It is the first hospital accreditation program in the United States that integrates the internationally recognized ISO 9001 Quality Management System with the Medicare Conditions of Participation, making it the first and only hospital accreditation program that requires continual quality improvement. As last reported, twenty-seven U.S. hospitals in twenty-two states have been accredited by DNV Healthcare using the NIAHO(SM) program in addition to other accreditation services. The World Health Organization (WHO), that rates American health care at thirty-seventh in the world, is actively promoting that concept of accreditation for all hospitals.

The good news is that, finally, after over forty

years of highly questionable service, the JC has some competition. The bad news appears to be that this new competition will seek to incorporate WHO quality health care standards along with the existing national quality standards that have proven to be less than effective where the doctor meets the patient—in our nation's hospitals and surgery centers.

I personally find this news greatly under-whelming.

PERSONAL PERSPECTIVE

I have judged other doctors in medical peer review and medical malpractice litigation. That is not an enjoyable way to occupy one's time, but I considered it an absolute responsibility if I were to consider myself a professional in every sense of that word.

Doctors must come to understand that to have a true profession they must create a true profession, and I just realized how often I have used the word *create* in this book, but that is exactly what is required. Doctors, and only doctors, can create a true medical profession by creating a true medical peer review system and that requires doctors to fairly judge other doctors regarding questionable patient care.

We have a long, disastrous history of trying to judge questionable patient care in every way but the right way. It's time we tried judging questionable patient care the right way—within the medical profession. When I judged another doctor I did not look upon that in such a simple way of one doctor judging another regarding how that doctor had treated a patient. I felt I had four professional responsibilities: to the other doctor, to the patient, to the profession, and to myself. Only by coming to understand that quadruple relationship was I able to volunteer my services as an expert witness in malpractice suits for patients I had never met, and this was the only means whereby I could participate in that grotesque system long enough to truly understand it.

Medical malpractice litigation is an abomination forced upon society by a medical profession incapable of providing society with the full fruit of a true profession, self-regulation of its members.

Most humans have a very harmful weakness seldom confronted; we look to have others do our dirty work for us, whenever and however possible. Doctors, and doctors alone, are the only ones who can ever properly judge the quality of health care and questionable patient care. It is time they shoulder their responsibility.

I am tired of every time I try to tell doctors of my peer review system they immediately begin to tell me why that system is "impossible." I am also tired of well-meaning "quality experts" telling the public how they are using the airline industry approach to improve the quality of health care, while they are actually bastardizing the most fruitful aspects of passenger (patient) safety by ignoring the most beneficial aspects of the airline industry's safety program.

My experience of over 2,700 flying hours as a US

Air Force navigator/bombardier and as a licensed single-engine aircraft pilot permits me to question this persistent misuse of information vital to full understanding. Airline pilots are tested annually, now in simulators, on as close to actual as possible in-flight emergency procedures. Don't you wish every surgeon could be forced to undergo such rigorous, lifelike safety training on a regular basis? Current quality health care experts only use those portions of the airline industry that fit their purpose.

Further explanation will prove helpful regarding this issue. The vast majority of all surgeries performed on any given day in all of the nation's operating rooms are "common and elective" procedures, meaning they are surgical or other invasive procedures performed on a routine basis and can be scheduled to fit the convenience of both doctor and patient. Emergency procedures and rare or seldom performed procedures would be the opposite. Also, all common and elective procedures have a current and acceptable standard of care, and although those standards of care can rarely be found, every medical procedure, in theory, has one.

Unfortunately for too many patients, far too many common and elective procedures are performed on patients using out-dated techniques. The airline industry's use of annual flight-testing in all manner of emergency procedures consistently identifies and eliminates out-dated flying procedures. The leading proponents of those seeking greater quality of health care and patient safety have been knowingly or unknowingly misusing that comparison for far too many years. We are, unfortunately, light-years away from ever enjoying all of the patient safety benefits in health care similar to those found for passenger safety in the airline industry.

I'm tired of meaningless articles like Dr. Blumenthal's survey on what is the reported current status of medical peer review in his hospital community, which received great public exposure and offers nothing of value to the quest for greater public safety in our health care system.

I'm tired of highly degreed people who have never, nor can ever, assume responsibility to treat another human being for a serious medical condition attempting to create theoretical quality of care guidelines that have no real chance of becoming truly useful in improving patient safety at the doctor-patient interface in every hospital in America. Policies and theories are of absolutely no value unless they can function in the real medical world within every hospital medical staff.

I'm tired of blatant lies being presented by the AMA, JC, AmHospitalAssoc., etc. and seeing none of them ever contested by the public's "watch-dog," all forms of the ever-present but seldom accountable media. Literature from Organized Medicine, JC, and the health care cottage industry is awash in untruths and half-truths and are consistently accepted on face value:

- Attorneys are not the cause of the medical malpractice crisis; doctors are the cause.

- JC does not, nor has it ever, set standards of care that can be utilized as such in any peer review or malpractice litigation hearing.

- The most beneficial safety aspects from the airline industry are not being used in the current patient safety efforts.

We, perhaps, will know real progress is being made when the various schools that teach individuals to be medical ethicists will begin to teach them that II in the AMA Principles of Medical Ethics includes medical peer review, and that is where the ethical foundation of that profession *must* begin.

Some will castigate me for this fit of anger. People everywhere should ask themselves, isn't it time for a fit of anger? When is anger appropriate? Even God gets angry. Patients are, and have been for far too long, needlessly dying in our hospitals while some will voice concern regarding a fit of anger by someone seeking to make a difference. Those quick to voice concern regarding my sudden outburst should spend some time talking *with* those survivors left to pick up the pieces of their life after seeing a loved one die a needless hospital death and later try to help make patient safety concerns better for others. *Twenty years later and* no *discernable improvement* should say it all.

Litmus test for the reality of medical peer review:

Gather as many thousands of practicing physicians under the same roof as possible and perform this test, if you dare. With every doctor seated, ask that any doctor who has:

- Peer reviewed the questionable patient care provided by another doctor in a formal and meaningful manner, seeking a clear conclusion, and/or

- Testified as an expert witness for a plaintiff (patient) in a medical malpractice litigation proceeding regarding questionable patient care (remember, there is no medical malpractice without expert witness testimony) please stand.

Instruct the audience that someone will come over to get sufficient data so as to avoid any "false positives." What percentage of doctors would anyone anticipate standing in an audience of thousands of practicing physicians under such a criteria?

I would anticipate less than 1 percent (so much for Dr. Blumenthal's survey).

I would then tell that audience of practicing physicians, "A great American philosopher once said, 'We has seen the enemy, and they is us!" Pogo.

Doctors are the best judges of other doctors, but doctors do not know how to judge other doctors. When you fail to fulfill the fundamentals of any endeavor, that endeavor is directed toward ultimate failure. Medical peer review is a tragic example of that truism and it is *not* true, because I say it is true. It is true, because it is true, because it is true.

Furthermore, you can never properly change our health care system by changing the cost and access aspects of that system alone. Anyone who looks at Education in America and thinks that the White House and Congress can create a health care system we can be proud of and benefit from as we should needs their head examined. They can always cut up the financial pie in order to move that system closer to a Socialistic form for the have-nots, but they can never create a health care system that will function at its best without properly addressing that system's organizational infrastructure and the quality of health care as determined by how we review questionable patient care.

Unfortunately, one example of how well recognized authorities can sometimes offer well-intentioned, but highly dubious, suggestions for health care change that, merely by their presence, those suggestions can become counterproductive.

Newt Gingrich, in his recent book Real Change provides one twenty-two-page chapter on how to transform health care in America. He concludes that chapter by describing in 2 ½ pages five major drivers and nine key strategies necessary for that transformational process to take place. I found Newt's theoretical plan for health care transformation to be comparable to a candidate for the title of Miss America wishing for World Peace.

Newt's second key strategy is:

Create *secure* electronic health records with expert systems to maximize accuracy, minimize errors, reduce inefficiencies, and improve care.

No one in their right mind could find fault with seeking that highly laudable goal However the reality is that this was written about the time Sarah Palin's personal e-mail was being invaded by a freshman at the University of Tennessee who just happened to be the son of a Democratic state legislator and while China, Russia and lord knows who else is hacking at every *secure* electronic system in our nation.

Fortunately for Newt and others like him, pontificating does not require one to provide the precise details on how to achieve the highly desirable fruits of their authoritarian musing.

How long will "experts" from every segment of our nation's intelligentsia continue to expound on how to change a huge, vital, social system none of them can describe in detail?

TALES FROM THE DARK SIDE

First, Do No Harm, The Cure for Medical Malpractice was published in 2005, and began with: "In Hilo, Hawaii, in 2001, Dr. Robert Ricketson, a surgeon, operated on a man to stabilize a disc injury in his spine. The titanium rod he needed to insert was not available in the operating room, so he reached for a nearby screwdriver, stuck it in the man's back, and sewed up the incision. Two days later, the screwdriver broke and the wound opened. After three more surgeries, by Dr. Ricketson trying to remedy the situation, the patient was left a bedridden, incontinent paraplegic. Soon after, he died.

"A nurse found the screwdriver in the trash. Shocked and outraged, she notified the patient's family. Why didn't anyone in the operating room notice this bizarre procedure and try to stop it? Why wasn't the hospital administration informed immediately so that corrective measures could be taken by a qualified orthopedist?

"At the time of the surgery, Dr. Ricketson had been charged with drug addiction and incompetence. His medical license had been suspended in Oklahoma and revoked in Texas. He was on probation in Hawaii for improper conduct. Was the highly touted physician's data bank inaccessible to the hospital administration? The data bank was created expressly for instances such as this one, to keep incompetent doctors from moving their practices from state to state.

"In this case, however, Dr. Ricketson's surgery seemingly was not monitored by his colleagues, despite the fact that he was a newcomer to Hilo. There is no record that anyone tried to stop his next three butcheries, yet the attending anesthesiologist and nurses must have been aware of them. Perhaps they didn't know what to do or were intimidated for some reason. Apparently, the hospital did not attempt to review Dr. Ricketson's conduct in the two years between the event and the malpractice trial, which was initiated by the patient's family."

Viewing health care in America is like looking at a full moon. We marvel at the beauty of the bright side while giving little thought to the dark side, unless astronauts are walking on it or an orthopedic surgeon is sticking a screwdriver into a patient's spinal column. Grotesque stories of medical negligence have been far too common for far too long, with no end seemingly in sight, while the search for better solutions offers little evidence of change for the better anytime soon.

Experience is the best teacher, and I have come by my deep understanding of medical malpractice and medical peer review through experiences as the second surgeon and/or malpractice expert witness to know that Dr. Ricketson's mindless surgical act was just one more example of far too many grossly negligent patient care events. Entering the practice of oral and maxillofacial surgery, I had not been prepared on how to assume the care of another doctor's patient who had been egregiously harmed. I guess they assume all doctors instinctively know to keep one's mouth shut and just do what you have to do.

Alice opened the door for me into the world of grossly negligent care with an injury as mundane as a simple fracture of her lower jaw received in a minor car accident. She was transferred from her small, rural hospital after a couple of days to a Madison medical center and placed under the care of a "head and neck specialist." Her broken jaw was the only injury that required treatment, and that treatment *should* have been simple surgery to set the fragments and wire her jaws together. Typically, for an uncomplicated case like this, a person should be in the hospital for one or two days after surgery and the fracture *should* have been healed in six weeks. Such was not to be the case for Alice.

A synopsis of Alice's introduction to negligent medical care exposes a lot more about the absence of functional regulation of the practice of medicine--if--one knows how to uncover it. Alice's surgeons (two brothers) made a debilitating mountain out of her traumatic molehill, as only two doctors treating a medical condition far out of their capability could do.

Alice was admitted to the hospital and had an excellent x-ray taken of her injury. That was the last acceptable form of medical care she was to receive for the next four months.

Surgeon #1 surgically treated her fracture, but negligently left a tooth in the line of fracture, whereby she became infected. She remained in the hospital for twelve days and was discharged still infected.

Several weeks later, Alice rolled over in bed and heard a "crack." Surgeon #2 had a totally inadequate x-ray taken at their clinic and readmitted her to the hospital. Alice was still infected, but not admitted as infected, and placed in a room with another patient. She had to walk down the hall to put warm compresses on her swollen jaw, thereby spreading her germs throughout that floor.

Near the end of her second twelve-day hospitalization, Surgeon #2 took her to the OR and "tightened her wires" holding her jaws together but doing nothing about the offending tooth in the line of fracture that was causing her prolonged infection. She remained under the care of Dumb and Dumber for a total of four months.

I first met Alice because she was appointed to see me to have an upper tooth extracted in the morning and was scheduled to see Surgeon #1 after lunch.

Because of her history of a recent jaw fracture, I was compelled to have a full jaw x-ray taken prior to removing her tooth. That was the first and only adequate post-op x-ray taken of her long-standing, complicated medical history with her injury.

I did what I would have wanted another surgeon to do for me in similar circumstances. I removed her upper tooth, called her surgeon, and sent my x-ray with her for her afternoon appointment, knowing Alice needed additional surgery. Surgeon #1 called me and asked my advice on how to treat her current condition.

I told him what I would do, and he said, "We can't do that. Will you treat her?"

I said, "Yes, have her and her husband return to my office, and please bring my x-ray."

That same evening, on the way home, I went to that hospital, because I was also a member of their medical staff, and reviewed her medical record and x-ray folder. It is difficult to describe my reaction upon seeing that two surgeons had done *nothing* right and *everything* wrong for four months and had *never* asked for help, and the patient was far worst then on the day of the original injury.

The next part of Alice's story exposes the real world of medical regulation within the "profession." After I had treated her complicated injury, I met with both surgeons and voiced my concern. Surgeon #2, the older brother, said they had done nothing wrong, but I could feel free to raise my concern to the medical staff leadership if I wished. I did, and the results should have been embarrassing to that medical staff, but no one was ever embarrassed.

The medical director's first question to me was, "Are you a troublemaker?" Readers should compare that belittling remark to the results of Dr. Blumenthal's specious survey, The Big Lie. Without telling Alice or her husband, but knowing that when questioning any level of review one is required to petition every level of the review system, I, as a hospital staff member, presented my concerns regarding her highly questionable care to every level of peer review, including the medical staff executive committee and the Sisterhood's head-shed in St. Louis. No fault was found at any level of that hospital's patient care review system.

One year later, at my request, Alice joined me to present our concerns to the JC review team leader both verbally and in writing. To no one's surprise, the JC gave that hospital a clean bill of health. A couple of years later (these things take time), both surgeons were found guilty of medical malpractice by a Wisconsin Medical Malpractice Patient Compensation Panel. Guess who the "bad guy" was in all of this?

During the entire process of peer review, through every level of that hospital's medical staff and administration, and with full details regarding all of her complications and protracted infirmary, not one person ever asked, "How is the patient?" But Alice was only the beginning.

One year after Alice's disastrous treatment, those same two surgeons treated another patient with a similar injury in a far worst manner but with the same infection results, in spite of having the assistance of a dentist and an infectious disease specialist, who was asked to assist, one must assume, because they anticipated that patient would also become infected after their original treatment. He did. By this time Alice's Surgeon #2 had been appointed Chief of Surgery at that hospital.

I practiced oral and maxillofacial surgery in a multi-man practice for eighteen years and am unaware that any of my other partners "attracted" patients negligently treated, who needed the services of a second surgeon as, for some unknown reason, I did. That is not a characteristic I sought or desired, but sometimes one is forced to deal with the hand they are dealt.

John will take the reader further into the insidious nature of the code of silence that has so tarnished the character of our medical profession throughout its history. John was a big man in his mid thirties with the unfortunate I.Q. of a five-year-old. His parents were senior citizens, and I was never able to meet his father, due to his age. John had a protruding "lantern-jaw" and was rapidly loosing his teeth because so few met in somewhat normal function. I told his mother I could surgically correct John's skeletal deformity, but John would have to have his jaws wired together for the six-week healing period. She feared that sounded too extreme and decided against my performing that surgery.

Unbeknownst to me, John's mother later heard that a plastic surgeon claimed to be able to do that surgery, and he only used elastic bands to hold the healing jaws together. Somehow, John's mother thought that sounded far more *humane*. John's story is horrifying for several reasons, but primarily because that surgeon was totally incompetent to perform that type of surgery, and the medical profession at that hospital, plus the chairman of the Plastic Surgery Department at the University of Wisconsin Medical School across town did everything they could to protect that surgeon's incompetence.

There were several different methods for surgically correcting John's deformity, and John's surgeon chose the method least often used and, by far, most difficult to perform. It is highly doubtful that John's surgeon had ever even attempted to perform that particular type of jaw surgery, which demands pre-formulated, precise, surgical, bony cuts and also demands meticulous preservation of the neuro-vascular bundle that supplies blood and nerve sensation to the lower jaw and lip.

John's first surgery was a surgical abomination that satisfied none of the specific surgical requirements necessary for a successful correction of his jaw deformity. John was readmitted to that hospital for additional, inadequate surgical attempts to reach some degree of post-operative stability five separate times with no success. After five months of incompetent care, John's mother consulted with a plastic surgeon at the University Hospital, whose recommendation was to use skin, muscle, and bone tissue flaps from John's upper chest for reconstruction on both sides of John's face. This heroic procedure would require John's jaws to be wired together for approximately six months.

A very embarrassed mother finally came to see me. She signed a paper transferring John's care over to me, and I told her John's surgery would require bone grafts taken from his hip and the surgery would take six hours. I underestimated that time by fifteen minutes, but John's surgically mutilated jaw was put into proper anatomical form, and his jaws were wired together for one week because I was able to use a form of external fixation that allowed him to freely open and close his mouth. John's permanent loss of sensation in his entire lower lip was a surgical defect I could not correct.

The remainder of John's story is a trip into the Dark Side of the medical profession. During John's many hospitalizations, I was later told by nurses, when other surgeons came on the floor to make rounds of their patients, John would frequently follow them from room to room and no one said a word to Big

John. The point of that story is that many doctors and nurses knew about John and his multiple admissions and problems, yet no one raised an alarm. John's surgeon had a long history of questionable patient care. I had previously removed the wires holding a young female's jaws together, because this same doctor had knowingly treated her for a fractured jaw after she had sustained a blow to the side of her face. The problem was she had previously had a jaw deformity surgically corrected and what appeared on an x-ray in the emergency room as a jaw fracture was merely the fully healed result of that earlier surgery. There is no question that John's surgeon had fraudulently treated her for a broken jaw he knew she did not have.

John's mother sued the first surgeon for malpractice, and as the second surgeon, I felt a responsibility to testify as to John's condition when I became responsible for his care and provide my professional opinion regarding his previous care. Professional and ethical conduct sank much deeper during the malpractice panel proceedings. The Chairman of the University of Wisconsin Plastic Surgery Department offered two blatant lies as sworn testimony in defense of that first surgeon. The lesser lie was that surgeon had been seeking consultations for help during John's many admissions and surgeries, when there was no evidence in the medical record to support that being fact.

The greater lie was that in his opinion John's surgeon had had surgical complications but was not guilty of negligent care. I testified that John had been the victim of surgical mutilation. John's first surgeon was found guilty of malpractice.

The Quality Chasm of health care lies on a foundation of professional deceit that has permeated the medical profession throughout its history and has been passively accepted as the Wall of Silence. I breeched that wall from the inside and from the vantage point of being the second surgeon responsible for correction, as best possible, the earlier harm. Long ago, I stopped being amazed at the professional misconduct one can so easily find when anyone seeks to question a doctor's questionable patient care, particularly in the system of malpractice litigation. Two additional cases will illustrate that point.

Because I had been forced by circumstances I believed to be out of my control to become the second surgeon in multiple questionable patient care events, and because I had seen firsthand the deception that was used and readily accepted within the medical profession in my community I made a, for me, life-changing decision. After much soul-searching and with the knowledge that there is *no* medical malpractice without the testimony of an expert witness, I decided to advertise my services as an expert witness outside my local community and my state. The world as I knew it changed forever. But I felt I needed to get deeper into that system in order to understand it, and understand it I do.

My naïve, hasty conclusion regarding the defendant doctor's response to the pending malpractice suit in the first out-of-state case I was asked to review illustrates how much I had to learn about the Dark Side of medical and surgical malpractice, and how close to home the Dark Side would be.

A middle-aged woman needed surgical correction of a mid-face deformity termed an anterior open-bite. In essence, there was a permanent space between her upper and lower front teeth, eliminating her ability to incise food. Recent advancements in facial surgery allowed oral surgeons with sufficient training and experience to surgically correct these deformities with great success. I had performed similar surgery numerous times.

Unfortunately, this lady had been referred by her dentist to an older oral surgeon who was on the part-time staff of the University of Ohio Department of Oral and Maxillofacial Surgery, but it remains uncertain even today his experience in performing this type surgical procedure. To make a long story short, his surgery was grossly inaccurate, the result was unacceptable, and his immediate response in attempting to correct his mistake(s) were bizarre.

She found a highly qualified surgeon who consented to re-operate her, but only after she wore braces for eighteen months and with the understanding that he would *not* testify against the first surgeon. There was no evidence that the University of Ohio

Department of Oral and Maxillofacial Surgery was ever contacted or became involved, even though the first surgeon was on their staff.

Her attorney sent me copies of the entire file, including x-rays, and my response to that attorney was, "I would expect this surgeon and his malpractice insurance company would just offer to settle this case without attempting to defend the indefensible." Wrong! That surgeon had been very active in the Great-Lakes Oral and Maxillofacial Surgery Association and was, in fact, that regional society's president. Thus, he had a long relationship with a man I knew well, the chairman of the Oral and Maxillofacial Surgery Department at the Wisconsin Medical School in Milwaukee.

That nameless "doctor" testified under oath in a deposition that he did *not* think the first surgeon had committed malpractice, and the lady's attorney felt they could not go to trial facing such testimony from such a source. To my knowledge, she never had her day in court, and the "Professions" had dodged another bullet.

I confronted that department chairman at a surgical conference, and his only response when I asked him, "How could you testify as you did?" was "I didn't have all of the records when I gave my deposition." That was a lie, and he rapidly walked away. I later attempted to bring this matter to the American Association of Oral and Maxillofacial Surgeons, but their response was that expert testimony is a matter of each practitioner's opinion, and they could not nor would not become involved.

One more case of a surgery department chairman and questionable patient care should be sufficient to shed some light on the Dark Side. The Chairman of the Department of Oral and Maxillofacial Surgery at the Harvard Medical School began seeing a patient with a jaw deformity in 1983, and that led to he and his surgery residents performing corrective surgery in 1985. All did not go well with that surgery, and the results led to a protracted period of poorly responded to complications.

That patient's attorney requested I review the records of that case in 1991, and yes, things move very slowly in the surgical malpractice litigation system. Also, that Department Chairman had since become Dean of Harvard Dental School. Massachusetts, at least then, required a plaintiff's (patient's) expert witness to provide a certifying letter listing questionable points so as to justify any litigation process to proceed. This is the body of the certifying letter I submitted in this case.

It is my opinion based on a reasonable degree of medical certainty that (patient) received sub-standard care and treatment by (doctor) during both the pre-surgical and post-surgical periods associated with his (blank) 1985 surgery and that sub-standard care did cause (patient) harm. I am qualified by training and experience to render such an opinion.

Opinion:

Pre-surgical aspects of sub-standard care:

- Inadequate and imprecise informed consent, including incorrect description of planned surgical procedure on both hospital consent form and medical record admit note and history and physical (H and P).

Post-surgical aspects of sub-standard care:

- Inadequate and imprecise documentation of multiple post-surgical complications in patient record.

- Inadequate and imprecise response to post-surgical complications, i.e

  1. Unsatisfactory result achieved by unilateral mandibular osteotomy (potential of this was anticipated).

  2. Unsatisfactory response to TMJ disorder which resulted from above.

  3. Inadequate response to Otitis Media complication.

4. Inadequate response to persistent post-surgical sinus infection complication.

Signed

That letter got the patient and his attorney (and I) into civil court in downtown Boston. David, however, in this case, could not overcome Goliath. I was the only expert witness for the patient. I do not know how many expert witnesses the Dean of Harvard Dental School called, but his potential list could have been endless.

Medical malpractice litigation requires the defense to establish a legally acceptable standard of care, the plaintiff (patient) and their attorney and expert witness to establish that the treatment received did *not* rise to an acceptable level, and for a jury of non-medical, lay "peers" to determine, did it or didn't it? Never bet against the doctor in medical malpractice cases. Yes, the Dean of Harvard Dental School won his case in downtown Boston, and yes, the patient probably continues to suffer some disability from that less-than-adequate surgery and post-operative care.

But something very insightful came out of that particular malpractice case, and to my chagrin, I did not realize its significance until much later, when it was too late. Litigation seeks to determine the standard of care of the treatment in question, since the medical profession has never been able to accomplish that much-needed determination. But that Chairman of the Department of Oral and Maxillofacial Surgery (at the time of surgery) was teaching his residents the standard of care for that specific procedure, was he not? Why was it necessary to call numerous other surgeons to establish a standard of care that chairman must have been in complete command of in order to teach it to others?

Medical malpractice litigation is a kabuki theater, and the public has been sold a lie, further distorted and tipped in the doctors' favor through medical malpractice tort reform. I, like all expert witnesses for the patients, was forced to endure being labeled a hired gun, when I was usually only compensated for my travel expenses and rarely ever paid for my time and expertise in preparation. That was because all of the patients I served were of modest means, and none, in my experience, won their case.

Every past and present leader of the professions must take responsibility for this disgrace. If they haven't spoken out against it, then they have condoned it, if not in some way participated in perpetuating it. I believe the only way to end this cycle of deceit is to examine in detail what is said by the experts on both sides openly, and challenge offerings that appear to contradict reason. Society will continue to get, from the medical profession, only what they demand, but it is up to us who know and understand that horrible system to help society know how they have been misused in the past and to know how to demand acceptable change.

The dark side of medical malpractice has a long history, and don't look to Organized Medicine to offer to change it. The only solution they continue to offer is medical malpractice tort reform, and that is just more of the same. Interested readers should go back to page two and reread Paul Starr's insightful depiction of when doctors had almost total control.

It has long been my intent to someday be considered one of the best friends our medical profession ever had. But first they must view themselves as far less than the beauty they should strive to become.

SUMMARY

All truth passes through three stages;
First, it is ridiculed
Second, it is violently opposed
Finally, it is accepted as being self-evident.

—Schopenhauer

Health care change is coming to America. Yet those who will take an active role in formulating that change cannot describe its current organizational configuration and have no interest in communicating with those who say they can. No one would attempt to dispute the fact that our health care system is replete with problems of every description. Now if only someone could describe them, but urgency to "do something" has overcome reason.

After over twenty years of countless, needless hospital deaths, with no evidence that rate equivalent to one fully loaded commercial airplane crash on a daily basis is being properly addressed, the powers-that-be fight over how to cut up that system's financial pie.

Nationally devised patient safety standards are like

the *Wizard of Oz*—just a lot of sound and fury, signifying nothing. When Toto pulled back the curtain, all could see just an old man pulling levers. The emptiness of the IOM To Err Is Human promise that is five years late and still empty is an apt comparison to that wizardless wizard. The same things lacking for the *Wizard of Oz* are the same things lacking in the fruitless attempts to create national standards for patient care. There are no clearly defined points of authority, responsibility, and accountability. Look at the emptiness of the NQF's Serious Reportable Events (SRE), reportable to whom and on whose authority can responses be anticipated? There ain't nothing there!

One can only understand how to regulate and control physician behavior by having experienced functioning within that elitist world. Doctors think differently than other people because they see themselves as different than other, *just* people. The surprise should come from the fact that people are surprised by that fact. Doctors, until the ever-growing governmental infringement on their world, lived, thought, and acted differently. It is very difficult for humans to easily cease from being "little human gods."

The future tragedy will come when we continue to diminish the allure of being a doctor until we are doctorless. If I were to speak to a large assembly of young people contemplating a career in medicine, I would say to them, "Don't choose a medical career unless you wish to assume responsibility for other humans." Most doctors have failed their profession and society. Most federal and state legislators have a greater failure. Doctors could never create a health care system worthy of our nation alone but were unable to recognize that fact. A health care system worthy of our nation can only be created by a positive collaboration between the existing components, all of who currently would rather fight than collaborate. We are all the losers.

My understanding of both medical malpractice and medical peer review became a perfect tool to take me into an understanding of that system's organizational infrastructure and equally important, from the perspective of a negligently harmed patient. The basic unit of all health care is one doctor and one patient. Equally important, all health care is local. It is from those two fundamental understandings where all considerations for real health care change should begin. Comparing how Abraham Flexner went about his great and highly successful task a hundred years ago and current efforts to do for the health care delivery system what he did for the medical education system would be hugely informative but would undermine the urgency.

The ability to cause great change gives one great power. The ability to live with the result of great change may be another matter. Not all change is beneficial. Therefore, will someone please help me understand, is it insensitive to say that only very foolish people would seek to change a huge, vital social system *none* of them can describe?

A CHALLENGE

To the medical profession and those organizations seeking to improve the quality of health care:

Given sufficient opportunity, I can provide a system of medical regulation that can organize the health care system in any state in the nation. May I anticipate a positive, open-minded acceptance to that challenge?

APPENDIX A

Health Care Time Line

1788   3,500 doctors, only 10% with a medical degree.

1859   Medical malpractice crisis throughout the nation.

1908–10 Abraham Flexner Report transforms medical education.

1910   AMA rules health care in America.

1941–45 WW II—GI Bill.

1950   Dawn of Modern Medicine.

1951   Joint Commission created by Organized Medicine.

1958   AMA—"Doctors will judge other doctors."

1965   Medicare and Medicaid—JC "deemed" by Congress.

1980   Department of Education—Carter Administration.

1986   Harvard Anesthesia Department—HCQIA-86 (peer review secret).

1987   Department of Defense peer review system.

1988   Joint Commission article in Wall Street Journal.

1996   IOM begins *Crossing the Quality Chasm* series.

1998   NQF established.

1999   DHHS-OIG-OEI "review" of Joint Commission.

2002   Joint Commission article in *Chicago Tribune.*

2003   AMA—malpractice standards set by the law and at the lowest hurdle.
         American College of Obstetrics and Gynecology peer review.

2004   IOM 7th book *Patient Safety in Crossing the Quality Chasm* series. (Fifty-three recommendations).

APPENDIX B

Institute of Medicine's Quality Chasm series

To Err Is Human: Building a Safer Health System 287 pages (2000)
9 Recommendations.

Crossing the Quality Chasm: A New Health System for the 21st Century 364 pages (2001)
13 Recommendations.

Leadership by Example: Coordinating Government Roles in Improving Health Care Quality 206 pages (2002)
8 Recommendations.

Health Professions Education: A Bridge to Quality 192 pages (2003)
10 Recommendations.

Priority Areas for National Action: Transforming Health Care Quality 160 pages (2003)
6 Recommendations.

Patient Safety: Achieving a New Standard for Care 528 pages (2004)
7 Recommendations.

53 TOTAL RECOMMENDATIONS

To Err Is Human:
Building a Safer Health System

Nine Recommendations

Recommendation 4.1: Congress should create a Center for Patient Safety within the Agency for Healthcare Research and Quality. This center should

- Set the national goals for patient safety, track progress in meeting these goals, and issue an annual report to the President and congress on patient safety; and

- Develop knowledge and understanding of errors in health care by developing a research agenda, funding Centers of Excellence, evaluating methods for identifying and preventing errors, and funding dissemination and communication activities to improve patient safety.

Recommendation 5.1: A nationwide mandatory reporting system should be established that provides for the collection of standardized information by state governments about adverse events that result in death or serious harm. Reporting should initially be required of hospitals and eventually be required of other institutional and ambulatory care delivery settings. Congress should

- Designate the National Forum for Health Care Quality Measurement and Reporting as the entity responsible for promulgating and maintaining a core set of reporting standards to be used by states, including a nomenclature and taxonomy for reporting;

- Require all health care organizations to report standardized information on a defined list of adverse events;

- Provide funds and technical expertise for state governments to establish or adapt their current error reporting systems to collect the standardized information, analyze it and conduct follow-up action as needed with health care organizations. Should a state choose not to implement the mandatory reporting system, the Department of Health and Human Services should be designated as the responsible entity; and

- Designate the Center for Patient Safety to:

  - Convene states to share information and expertise, and to evaluate alternative approaches taken for implementing reporting programs, identify best practices for implementation, and assess the impact of state programs; and

  - Receive and analyze aggregate reports from states to identify persistent safety issues that require more intensive analysis and/or a broader-based response (e.g., designing prototype systems or requesting a response by agencies, manufacturers or others).

Recommendation 5.2: The development of voluntary reporting efforts should be encouraged. The Center for Patient Safety should

- Describe and disseminate information on existing voluntary reporting programs to encourage greater participation in them and track the development of new reporting systems as they form;

- Convene sponsors and users of external reporting systems to evaluate what works and what does not work well in the programs, and ways to make them more effective.

- Periodically assess whether additional efforts are needed to address gaps in information to improve patient safety and to encourage health care organizations to participate in voluntary reporting programs; and

- Fund and evaluate pilot projects for reporting systems, both within individual health care organizations and collaborative efforts among health care organizations.

Recommendation 6.1: Congress should pass legislation to extend peer review protections to data related to patient safety and quality improvement that are collected and analyzed by health care organizations for internal use or shared with others solely for purposes of improving safety and quality.

Recommendation 7.1: Performance standards and expectations for health care organizations should focus greater attention on patient safety.

- Regulators and creditors should require health care organizations to implement meaningful patient safety programs with defined executive responsibility.

- Public and private purchasers should provide incentives to health care organizations to demonstrate continuous improvement in patient safety.

Recommendation 7.2: Performance standards and expectations for health professionals should focus greater attention on patient safety.

- Health professional licensing bodies should

    - Implement periodic reexaminations and relicensing of doctors, nurses, and other key providers, based on both competence and knowledge of safety practices; and

- Work with certifying and credentialing organizations to develop more effective methods to identify unsafe providers and take action.

• Professional societies should make a visible commitment to patient safety by establishing a permanent committee dedicated to safety improvement. This committee should

- Develop a curriculum on patient safety and encourage its adoption into training and certification requirements;

- Disseminate information on patient safety to members at special sessions at annual conferences, journal articles and editorials, newsletters, publications and websites on a regular basis;

- Recognize patient safety considerations in practice guidelines and in standards related to the introduction and diffusion of new technologies, therapies, and drugs;

- Work with the Center for Patient Safety to develop community-based, collaborative initiatives for error reporting and analysis and implementation of patient safety improvements; and

- Collaborate with other professional societies and disciplines in a national summit on the professional's role in patient safety.

Recommendation 7.3: The Food and Drug Administration (FDA) should increase attention to the safe use of drugs in both pre and post-marketing processes through the following actions.

- Develop and enforce standards for the design of drug packaging and labeling that will maximize safety in use;

- Require pharmaceutical companies to test (using FDA-approved methods) proposed drug names to identify and remedy potential sound-alike and look-alike confusion with existing drug names; and

- Work with physicians, pharmacists, consumers and others to establish appropriate responses to problems identified through post-marketing surveillance, especially for concerns that are perceived to require immediate response to protect the safety of patients.

Recommendation 8.1: Health care organizations and the professionals affiliated with them should make continually improved patient safety a declared and serious aim by establishing patient safety programs with a defined executive responsibility. Patient safety programs should: (1) provide strong, clear, and visible attention to safety; implement non-punitive systems for reporting and analyzing errors within their organizations; (2) incorporate well-understood safety principles, such as, standardizing and simplifying equipment, supplies, and processes; and (3) establish interdisciplinary team training programs, such as simulation, that incorporate proven methods of team management.

Recommendation 8.2: Health care organizations should implement proven medication safety practices.

Crossing The Quality Chasm: A New Health System for the 21st Century

Thirteen Recommendations

Recommendation 1: All health care organizations, professional groups, and private and public purchasers should adopt as their explicit purpose to continually reduce the burden of illness, injury, and disability, and to improve the health and functioning of the people of the United States.

Recommendation 2: All health care organizations, professional groups, and private and public purchasers should pursue six major aims; specifically, health care should be safe, effective, patient-centered, timely, efficient, and equitable.

Recommendation 3: Congress should continue to authorize and appropriate funds for, and the Department of Health and Human Services should move forward expeditiously with the establishment of, monitoring and tracking processes for use in evaluating the progress of the health system in pursuit of the above-cited aims of safety, effectiveness, patient-centeredness, timeliness, efficiency, and equity. The Secretary of the Department of Health and Human Services should report annually to congress and the President on the quality of care provided to the American people.

Recommendation 4: Private and public purchasers, health care organizations, clinicians, and patients should work together to redesign health care processes in accordance with the following rules:

1. Care based on continuous healing relationships. Patients should receive care whenever they need it and in many forms, not just face-to-face visits. This rule implies that the health care system should be responsive at all times (24 hours a day, every day) and that access to care should be provided over the Internet, by telephone, and by other means in addition to face-to-face visits.

2. Customization based on patient needs and values. The system of care should be designed to meet the most common types of needs, but have the capability to respond to individual patient choices and preferences.

3. The patient as the source of control. Patients should be given the necessary information and the opportunity to exercise the degree of control they choose over health care decisions that affect them. The health system should be able to accommodate differences in patient preferences and encourage shared decision making.

4. Shared knowledge and the free flow of information. Patients should have unfettered access to their own medical information and to clinical knowledge. Clinicians and patients should communicate effectively and share information.

5. Evidence-based decision making. Patients should receive care based on the best available scientific knowledge. Care should not vary illogically from clinician to clinician or from place to place.

6. Safety as a system property. Patients should be safe from injury caused by the care system. Reducing risk and ensuring safety require greater attention to systems that help prevent and mitigate errors.

7. The need for transparency. The health care system should make information available to patients and their families that allows them to make informed decisions when selecting a health plan, hospital, or clinical practice, or choosing among alternative treatments. This should include information describing the system's performance on safety, evidence-based practice, and patient safety satisfaction.

8. Anticipation of needs. The health system should anticipate patient needs, rather than simply reacting to events.

9. Continuous decrease in waste. The health system should not waste resources or patient time.

10. Cooperation among clinicians. Clinicians and institutions should actively collaborate and communicate to ensure an appropriate exchange of information and coordination of care.

Recommendation 5: The Agency for Healthcare Research and Quality should identify not fewer than 15 priority conditions, taking into account frequency of occurrence, health burdens, and resource use. In collaboration with the National Quality Forum, the agency should convene stakeholders, including purchasers, consumers, health care organizations, professional groups, and others, to develop strategies, goals, and action plans for achieving substantial improvements in quality in the next 5 years for each of the priority conditions.

Recommendation 6: Congress should establish a Health Care Quality Innovation Fund to support projects targeted at (1) achieving the six aims of safety, effectiveness, patient-centeredness, timeliness, efficiency, and equity; and/or (2) producing substantial improvements in quality for the priority conditions. The fund's resources should be invested in projects that will produce a public-domain portfolio of programs, tools, and technologies of widespread applicability.

Recommendation 7: The Agency for Healthcare Research and Quality and private foundations should convene a series of workshops involving representatives from health care and other industries and the research community to identify, adapt, and implement state-of-the-art approaches to addressing the following challenges:

- Redesign of care processes based on best practices

- Use of information technologies to improve access to clinical information and support clinical decision making

- Knowledge and skills management

- Development of effective teams

- Coordination of care across patient conditions, services, and settings over time

- Incorporation of performance and outcome measurements for improvement and accountability

Recommendation 8: The Secretary of the Department of Health and Human Services should be given the responsibility and necessary resources to establish and maintain a comprehensive program aimed at making scientific evidence more useful and accessible to clinicians and patients. In developing this program, the Secretary should work with federal agencies and in collaboration with professional and health care associations, the academic and research communities, and the National Quality Forum and other organizations involved in quality measurement and accountability.

Recommendation 9: Congress, the executive branch, leaders of health care organizations, public and private purchasers, and health informatics associations and vendors should make a renewed national commitment to building an information infrastructure to support health care delivery, consumer health, quality measurement and improvement, public accountability, clinical and health services research, and clinical education. This commitment should lead to the elimination of most handwritten clinical data by the end of the decade.

Recommendation 10: Private and public purchasers should examine their current payment methods to remove barriers that currently impede quality improvement, and to build in stronger incentives for quality enhancement.

Recommendation 11: The Health Care Financing Administration and the Agency for Healthcare Research and Quality, with input from private payers, health care organizations, and clinicians, should develop a research agenda to identify, pilot test, and evaluate various options for better aligning current payment methods with quality improvement goals.

Recommendation 12: A multidisciplinary summit of leaders within the health professions should be held to discuss and develop strategies for (1) restructuring clinical education to be consistent with the principles of the 21st-century health system throughout the continuum of undergraduate, graduate, and continuing education for medical, nursing, and other professional training programs; and (2) assessing the implications of these changes for provider credentialing programs, funding, and sponsorship of education programs for health professionals.

Recommendation 13: The Agency for Healthcare Research and Quality should fund research to evaluate how the current regulatory and legal systems (1) facilitate or inhibit the changes needed for the 21st-century health care delivery system, and (2) can be modified to support health care professionals and organizations that seek to accomplish the six aims set forth in Chapter 2.

Leadership by Example: Coordinating Government Roles in Improving Health Care Quality

Eight Recommendations

Recommendation 1: The federal government should assume a strong leadership position in driving the health care sector to improve the safety and quality of health care services provided to the approximately 100 million beneficiaries of the six major government health care programs. Given the leverage of the federal government, this leadership will result in improvements in the safety and quality of health care provided to all Americans.

Recommendation 2: The federal government should take maximal advantage of its unique position as regulator, health care purchaser, health car provider, and sponsor of applied health services research to set quality standards for the health care sector. Specifically:

1. Regulatory processes should be used to establish clinical data reporting requirements applicable to all six major government health care programs.

2. All six major government health care programs should vigorously pursue purchasing strategies that encourage

the adoption of best practices through the release of public domain comparative quality data and the provision of financial and other rewards to providers that achieve high levels of quality.

3. Not only should health care delivery systems operated by the public programs continue to serve as laboratories for the development of innovative 21st-century care delivery models, but much greater emphasis should be placed on the dissemination of findings and, in the case of information technology, the creation of public-domain products.

4. Applied health services research should be expanded and should emphasize the development of knowledge, tools, and strategies that can support quality enhancement in a wide variety of settings.

Recommendation 3: Congress should direct the Secretaries of the Department of Health and Human Services (DHHS), Department of Defense (DOD), and Department of Veterans Affairs (VA) to work together to establish standardized performance measures across the government programs, as well as public reporting requirements for clinicians, institutional providers, and health plans in each program. These requirements should be implemented for all six major government health care programs and should be applied fairly and equitably across various financing and delivery options within those programs. The standardized measurement and reporting activities should replace the many performance measurement activities currently under way in the various government programs.

Recommendation 4: The Quality Interagency Coordination (QuIC) Task Force should promulgate standardized sets of performance measures for 5 common health conditions in fiscal year (FY) 2003 and another 10 sets in FY 2004.

Each government health care program should pilot test the first 5 sets of measures between FY 2003 and FY 2005 in a limited number of sites. These pilot tests should

1. include the collection of patient-level data and the public release of comparative performance reports.

2. All six government programs should prepare for full implementation of the 15-set performance measurement and reporting system by FY 2008. The government health care programs that provide services through the private sector (i.e., Medicare, Medicaid, the State Children's Health Insurance Program (SCHIP), and portions of DOD (TRICARE) should inform participating providers that submission of the audited patient-level data necessary for performance measurement will be required for continued participation in FY 2007. The government health care programs that provide services directly (i.e., the Veterans Health Administration (VHA), the remainder of DOD TRICARE, and the Indian Health Services (IHS) should begin work immediately to ensure that they have the information technology capabilities to produce the necessary data.

Recommendation 5: The federal government should take steps immediately to encourage and facilitate the development of the information technology infrastructure that is critical to health care quality and safety enhancement, as well as to many of the nation's other priorities, such as bioterrorism surveillance, public health, and research.

Specifically:

1. Congress should consider potential options to facilitate rapid development of a national health information

infrastructure, including tax credits, subsidized loans, and grants.

2. Government health care programs that deliver services through the private sector-Medicare, Medicaid, the State Children's Health Insurance Program (SCHIP), and a portion of Department of Defense (DOD) TRICARE-should adopt both market-based and regulatory options to encourage investment in information technology. Such options might include enhanced or more rapid payments to providers capable of submitting computerized clinical data, a requirement for certain information technology capabilities as a condition of participation and direct grants.

3. The Veterans Health Administration (VHA), DOD TRICARE, and the Indian Health Service (HIS) should continue implementing clinical and administrative information systems that enable the retrieval of clinical information across their programs and can communicate directly with each other. Whenever possible, the software and intellectual property developed by these three government programs should rely on Web-based language and architecture and be made available in the public domain.

Recommendation 6: Starting in FY 2008, each government health care program should make comparative quality reports and data available in the public domain. The program should provide for access to these reports and data in ways that meet the needs of various users, provided that patient privacy is protected.

Recommendation 7: The government health care programs, working with the Agency for Healthcare Research and Quality (AHRQ), should establish a mechanism for pooling performance measurement data across programs in a data repository. Contributions of data from private-sector insurance programs should be encouraged provided such data meet certain standards for validity and reliability. Consumers, health care professionals, planners, purchasers, regulators, public health officials, researchers, and others should be afforded access to the repository, provided that patient privacy is protected.

Recommendation 8: The government health care programs should work together to develop a comprehensive health services research agenda that will support the quality enhancement processes of all programs. The Quality Interagency Coordination (QuIC) Task Force (or some similar interdepartmental structure with representation from each of the government health care programs and the Agency for Healthcare Research and Quality (AHRQ) should be provided the authority and resources needed to carry out this responsibility. This agenda for fiscal years (FY) 2003–2005 should support the following:

1. Establishment of core sets of standardized performance measures

2. Ongoing evaluation of the impact of the use of standardized performance measurement and reporting by the six major government health care programs

3. Development and evaluation of specific strategies that can be used to improve the federal government's capability to leverage its purchaser, regulator, and provider roles to enhance quality.

4. Monitoring of national progress in meeting the six national quality aims (safety, effectiveness, patient-centeredness, timeliness, efficiency, and equity)

Health Professions Education: A Bridge to Quality

Ten Recommendations

Recommendation 1: DHHS and leading foundations should support an interdisciplinary effort focused on developing a common language with the ultimate aim of achieving consensus across the health professions on a core set of competencies that includes patient-centered care, interdisciplinary teams, evidence-based practice, quality improvement and information.

Recommendation 2: DHHS should provide a forum and support for a series of meetings involving the spectrum of oversight organizations across and within the disciplines. Participants in these meetings would be charged with developing strategies for incorporating a core set of competencies into oversight activities, based on definitions shared across the professions. These meetings would actively solicit the input of health professions associations and the education community.

Recommendation 3: Building upon previous efforts, accreditation bodies should move forward expeditiously to revise their standards so that programs are required to demonstrate––through process and outcome measures—that they educate students in both academic and continuing education programs in how to deliver patient care using a core set of competencies. In so doing, these bodies should coordinate their efforts.

Recommendation 4: All health professions boards should move toward requiring licensed health professionals to demonstrate periodically their ability to deliver patient care—as defined by the five competencies identified by the committee—through direct measures of technical competence, patient assessment, evaluation of patient outcomes, and other evidence-based assessment methods. These boards should simultaneously evaluate the different assessment methods.

Recommendation 5: Certification bodies should require their certificate holders to maintain their competence throughout the course of their careers by periodically demonstrating their ability to deliver patient care that reflects the five competencies, among other requirements.

Recommendation 6: Foundations, with support from education and practice organizations, should take the lead in developing and funding regional demonstration learning centers, representing partnerships between practice and education. These centers should leverage existing innovative organizations and be state-of-the-art training settings focused on teaching and assessing the five core competencies.

Recommendation 7: Through Medicare demonstration projects, the Center for Medicare and Medicaid Services (CMS) should take the lead in funding experiments that will enable and create incentives for health professionals to integrate interdisciplinary approaches into educational or practice settings with the goal of providing a training ground for students and clinicians that incorporates the five core competencies.

Recommendation 8: The Agency for Healthcare Research and Quality (AHRQ) and private foundations should support ongoing research projects addressing the five core competencies and their association with individual and population health, as well as research related to the link between the competencies and evidence-based education. Such projects should involve researchers across two or more disciplines.

Recommendation 9: AHRQ should work with a representative group of health care leaders to develop measures reflecting the core set of competencies, set national goals for improvement, and issue a report to the public evaluating progress toward these goals. AHRQ should issue the first report, focused on clinical educational institutions, in 2005 and produce annual reports thereafter.

Recommendation 10: Beginning in 2004, a biennial interdisciplinary summit should be held involving health care leaders in education, oversight processes, practice, and other areas. This summit should focus on both reviewing progress against explicit targets and setting goals for the next phase with regard to the five competencies and other areas necessary to prepare professionals for the 21st century health system.

Priority Areas for National Action: Transforming Health Care Quality

6 Recommendations

Recommendation 1: The committee recommends that the priority areas collectively:

- Represent the U.S. population's health care needs across the lifespan, in multiple health care settings involving many types of health care professionals.

- Extend across the full spectrum of health care, from keeping people well and maximizing overall health; to providing treatment to cure people of disease and health problems as often as possible; to assisting people who become chronically ill to live longer, more productive and comfortable lives; to providing dignified care at the end of life that is respectful of the values and preferences of individuals and their families.

Recommendation 2: The committee recommends use of the following criteria for identifying priority areas:

- Impact—the extent of the burden—disability, mortality, and economic costs—imposed by a condition, including effects on patients, families, communities, and societies.

- Improvability- the extent of the gap between current practice and evidence-based best practice and the likelihood that the gap can be closed and conditions improved through change in an area; and the opportunity to achieve dramatic improvements in the six national quality aims identified in the Quality Chasm report (safety, effectiveness, patient-centeredness, timeliness, efficiency and equity).

- Inclusiveness—the relevance of an area to a broad range of individuals with regard to age, gender, socioeconomic status, and ethnicity/race (equity); the generalizability of associated quality improvement strategies to many types of conditions and illnesses across the spectrum of health care (representativeness); and the breadth of change effected through such strategies across a range of health care settings and providers (reach).

Recommendation 3: The committee recommends that DHHS, along with other public and private entities, focus on the following priority areas for transforming health care:

- Care coordination (cross-cutting)

- Self-management/health literacy (cross-cutting)

- Asthma—appropriate treatment for persons with mild/moderate persistent asthma

- Cancer screening that is evidence-based—focus on colorectal and cervical cancer

- Children with special health care needs

- Diabetes—focus on appropriate management of early disease

- End of life with advanced organ system failure—focus on congestive heart failure and chronic obstructive pulmonary disease

- Frailty associated with old age—preventing falls and pressure ulcers, maximizing function, and developing advanced care plans

- Hypertension—focus on appropriate management of early disease

- Immunization—children and adults

- Ischemic heart disease—prevention, reduction of recurring events, and optimization of functional capacity

- Major depression—screening and treatment

- Medication management—preventing medication errors and overuse of antibiotics

- Nosocomial infections—prevention and surveillance

- Pain control in advanced cancer

- Pregnancy and childbirth—appropriate prenatal and intrapartum care

- Severe and persistent mental illness—focus on treatment in the public sector

- Stroke—early intervention and rehabilitation

- Tobacco dependence treatment in adults

- Obesity (emerging area)

Recommendation 4: The committee recommends that the Agency for Healthcare Research and Quality (AHRQ), in collaboration with other private and public organizations, be responsible for continuous assessment of progress and updating of the list of priority areas. These responsibilities should include:

- Developing and improving data collection and measurement systems for assessing the effectiveness of quality improvement efforts.

- Supporting the development and dissemination of valid, accurate, and reliable standardized measures of quality.

- Measuring key attributes and outcomes and making this information available to the public.

- Revising the selection criteria and the list of priority areas.

- Reviewing the evidence base and results, and deciding on updated priorities every 3 to 5 years.

- Assessing changes in the attributes of society that affect health and health care and could alter the priority of various areas.

- Disseminating the results of strategies for quality improvement in the priority areas.

Recommendation 5: The committee recommends that data collection in the priority areas:

- Go beyond the usual reliance on disease—and procedure-based information to include data on the health and functioning of the U.S. population.

- Cover relevant demographic and regional groups, as well as the population as a whole, with particular emphasis on identifying disparities in care.

- Be consistent within and across categories to ensure accurate assessment and comparison of quality enhancement efforts.

Recommendation 6: The committee recommends that the congress and the Administration provide the necessary support for the ongoing process of monitoring progress in the priority areas and updating the list of areas. This support should encompass:

- The administration costs borne by AHRQ.

- The costs of developing and implementing data collection mechanisms and improving the capacity to measure results.

- The costs of investing strategically in research aimed at developing new scientific evidence on interventions that improve the quality of care and at creating additional accurate, valid, and reliable standardized measures of quality.

Patient Safety:
Achieving a New Standard for Care

7 Recommendations

Recommendation 1: Americans expect and deserve safe care. Improved information and data systems are needed to support efforts to make patient safety a standard of care in hospitals, in doctors' offices, in nursing homes, and in every other health care setting. All health care organizations should establish comprehensive patient safety systems that:

- Provide immediate access to complete patient information and decision support tools (e.g., alerts, reminders) for clinicians and their patients.

- Capture information on patient safety—including both adverse events and near misses—as a by-product of care and use this information to design even safer care delivery systems.

Recommendation 2: A national health information infrastructure—a foundation of systems, technology, applications, standards, and policies—is required to make patient safety a standard of care.

- The federal government should facilitate deployment of the national health information infrastructure through the provision of targeted financial support and the ongoing promulgation and maintenance of standards for data that support patient safety.

- Health care providers should invest in electronic health record systems that possess the key capabilities necessary to provide safe and effective care and to enable the continuous redesign of care processes to improve patient safety.

- Clinical terminologies. The federal government should move expeditiously to identify a core set of well-integrated, non-redundant clinical terminologies for clinical care, quality improvement, and patient safety reporting. Revisions, extensions, and additions to the codes should be compatible with, yet go beyond, the federal government's initiative to integrate all federal reporting systems.

  - AHRQ should undertake a study of the core terminologies, supplemental terminologies, and standards mandated by the Health Insurance Portability and Accountability Act to identify areas of overlap and gaps in the terminologies to address patient safety data requirements. The study should begin by convening domain experts to develop a process for ensuring comprehensive coverage of the terminologies for the 20 IOM priority areas.

  - The National Library of Medicine should provide support for the accelerated completion of RxNORM2 for clinical drugs. The National Library of Medicine also should develop high-quality mappings among the core terminologies and supplemental terminologies identified by the CHI and NCVHS.

- Knowledge representation. The federal government should provide support for the accelerated development of knowledge representation standards to facilitate effective use of decision support in clinical information systems.

- The National Library of Medicine should provide support for the development of standards for evidence-based knowledge representation.

- AHRQ, in collaboration with the National Institutes of Health, the Food and Drug Administration, and other agencies, should provide support for the development of a generic guideline representation model for use in representing clinical guidelines in a computer-executable format that can be employed in decision support tools.

Recommendation 3: Congress should provide clear direction, enabling authority, and financial support for the establishment of national standards for data that support patient safety. Various government agencies will need to assume major new responsibilities and additional support will be required. Specifically:

- The Department of Health and Human Services (DHHS) should be given the lead role in establishing and maintaining a public-private partnership for the promulgation of standards for data that support patient safety.

- The Consolidated Health Informatics (CHI) initiative, in collaboration with the National Committee on Vital and Health Statistics (NCVHS), should identify data standards appropriate for national adoption and gaps in existing standards that need to be addressed. The membership of NCVHS should continue to be broad and diverse, with adequate representation of all stakeholders, including consumers, state governments, professional groups, and standard-setting bodies.

- The Agency for Healthcare Research and Quality

(AHRQ), in collaboration with the National Library of Medicine and others, should (1) provide administrative and technical support for the CHI and NCVHS efforts; (2) ensure the development of implementation guides, certification procedures, and conformance testing for all data standards; (3) provide financial support and oversight for development activities to fill gaps in data standards; and (4) coordinate activities and maintain a clearinghouse of information in support of national data standards and their implementation to improve patient safety.

- The National Library of Medicine should be designated as the responsible entity for distributing all national clinical terminologies that relate to patient safety and for ensuring the quality of terminology mappings.

Recommendation 4: The lack of comprehensive standards for data to support patient safety impedes private-sector investment in information technology and other efforts to improve patient safety. The federal government should accelerate the adoption of standards for such data by pursuing the following efforts:

- Clinical data interchange standards. The federal government should set an aggressive agenda for the establishment of standards for the interchange of clinical data to support patient safety. Federal financial support should be provided to accomplish this agenda.

  - After ample time for provider compliance, government health care programs should incorporate into their contractual and regulatory requirements standards already approved by the secretaries of DHHS, the Veterans Administration, and the Department of Defense (i.e., the HL7 version 2.x series for clinical data messaging, DICOM for medical imaging, IEEE 1073 for medical devices, LOINC for laboratory test results, and NCPCP Script for prescription data).

- AHRQ should provide support for (1) accelerated completion (within 2 years) of HL7 version 3.0; (2) specifications for the H7 Clinical Document Architecture and implementation guides; and (3) analysis of alternative methods for addressing the need to support patient safety by instituting a unique health identifier for individuals, such as implementation of a voluntary unique health identifier program.

Recommendation 5: All health care settings should establish comprehensive patient safety programs operated by trained personnel within a culture of safety. These programs should encompass (1) case finding—identifying system failures, (2) analysis—understanding the factors that contribute to system failures, and (3) system redesign—making improvements in care processes to prevent errors in the future. Patient safety programs should invite the participation of patients and their families and be responsive to their inquiries.

Recommendation 6. The federal government should pursue a robust applied research agenda on patient safety, focused on enhancing knowledge, developing tools, and disseminating results to maximize the impact of patient safety systems. AHRQ should play a lead role in coordinating this research agenda among federal agencies (e.g., the National Library of Medicine) and the private sector. The research agenda should include the following:

- Knowledge generation
  - High-risk patients—Identify patients at risk for medication errors, nosocomial infections, falls, and other high-risk events.

  - Near-miss incidents—Test the causal continuum assumption (that near misses and adverse events are causally related), develop and test a recovery taxonomy, and extend the current individual human error/recovery models to team-based errors and recoveries.

  - Hazard analysis—Assess the validity and efficiency of integrating retrospective techniques (e.g., incident analysis) with prospective techniques.

  - High-yield activities—Study the cost/benefit of various approaches to patient safety, including analysis of reporting systems for near misses and adverse events.

  - Patient roles—Study the role of patients in the prevention, early detection, and mitigation of harm due to errors.

- Tool development
  - Early detection capabilities—Develop and evaluate various methods for employing data-driven triggers to detect adverse drug errors, nosocomial infections, and other high-risk events (e.g., patient falls, decubitus ulcers, complications of blood product transfusions).

- Prevention capabilities—Develop and evaluate point-of-care decision support to prevent errors of omission or commission.

- Data mining techniques—Identify and develop data mining techniques to enhance learning from regional and national patient safety databases. Apply natural language processing techniques to facilitate the extraction of patient safety-related concepts from text documents and incident reports.

• Dissemination—Deploy knowledge and tools to clinicians and patients.

Recommendation 7: AHRQ should develop an event taxonomy and common report format for submission of data to the national patient safety database. Specifically:

• The event taxonomy should address near misses and adverse events, cover errors of both omission and commission, allow for the designation of primary and secondary event types for cases in which more than one factor precipitated the adverse event, and be incorporated into SNOMED CT.

• The standardized report format should include the following:

- A standardized minimum set of data elements.

- Data necessary to calculate a risk assessment index for determining prospectively the probability of an event and its severity.

- A free-text narrative of the event.

- Data necessary to support use of the Eindhoven

Classification Model—Medical Version for classifying root causes, including expansions for (1) recovery factors associated with near-miss events, (2) corrective actions taken to recover from adverse events, and (3) patient outcome/functional status as a result of those corrective actions.

- A free-text section for lessons learned as a result of the event.

- Clinical documentation of the patient context.

• The taxonomy and report format should be used by the federal reporting system integration project in the areas for basic domain, event type, risk assessment, and causal analysis but should provide for more extensive support for patient safety research and analysis (Department of Health and Human Services, 2002).

APPENDIX C

Disclaimer
Scientific Elements Standard of Care

Many surgeons qualified to perform double jaw surgery will find fault with Appendix C.

That is precisely its intent!

Colleagues must review and improve treatment specific standard of care check lists within their personal areas of expertise.

In that manner, out-dated treatment protocols can be recognized and eliminated.

In that manner, current and acceptable treatment protocols can become the norm.

All medical treatment falls under (4) possible categories:

1. Current and acceptable.

2. Out-dated.

3. Advanced (cutting-edge).

4. Grossly irrational negligent care (this too occurs).

Donald J. Palmisano, MD, JD, AMA Past President stated: "The law does not require the best. The law requires a minimally acceptable level of care, thus my analogy to the low hurdle."

IRPR system will strive to make a current and acceptable standard of care the norm.

Four classes of medical practitioners can be identified to be practicing medicine within the zone of patient care represented between a current and acceptable standard of care and treatment acceptable at the "low hurdle":

1. Practitioners unqualified to retain a medical license.

2. Practitioners marginally qualified whose practice should be limited to their ability.

3. Practitioners using out-dated patient care techniques.

4. Qualified practitioners who make a human error which can only be recognized by a review of that doctor's patient care track record.

Scientific Elements—Standard of Care Bi-Maxillary Surgery of Facial Deformity

LeFort I Maxillary Ostectomy and
Bi-lateral Mandibular Osteotomy

Diagnosis:

Maxillary and mandibular dental models trimmed in centric relationship.

Models mounted on an anatomical articulator.

Cephalometric x-rays with tracings depicting surgery.

Panorex x-ray.

Orthodontic consult as necessary.

Treatment Plan:

Maxillary Hyperplasia requires ostectomy and superior repositioning of maxilla.

Mandibular bi-lateral sagittal-split osteotomies with advancement.

Rigid bi-maxillary skeletal fixation.

Model surgery and fabrication of intermediate and final occlusal splints.

Current and past medical history:

Rule-out medical contra-indication to surgery.

Identify need for medical consultation and over-sight.

Routine pre-op laboratory including t/c for possible transfusion.

Operating room pre-surgical patient disposition:

Nasal intubation - general anesthesia.

Naso-gastric tube.

G-U catheterization, p.r.n.

Sterile drape isolation of oral surgical field.

Upper body slightly elevated for hemostasis.

Oral cavity and upper respiratory region suctioned dry and packed with sterile packs.

Circulating staff instructed regarding pack count and blood loss determination.

Maxillary ostectomy surgery:

Bi-lateral maxillary mucosa injected—local anesthesia with epinephrine for hemostasis.

Muco-periosteal incision in buccal sulcus from left 1st molar region to right 1st molar region.

Muco-periosteal flap reflected exposing lateral maxillary wall.

Left intra-nasal mucosa reflected anterior to posterior.

Vertical reference lines cut into lateral bony wall for repositioning reference.

Horizontal osteotomies through lateral maxillary and nasal walls from anterior to posterior.

Second horizontal osteotomies through lateral maxillary and nasal walls from anterior to posterior for desired ostectomy and vertical repositioning.

Osteotome and mallet used for maxillary/pterygoid separation.

Similar osteotomies performed on right maxilla.

Maxillary down-fracture.

Free mobilization of dental segment of maxilla obtained.

Mobilized maxillary dentition fixed to mandibular dentition using intermediate occlussal splint.

Mandible counter-rotated to desired maxillary post-surgical position.

Rigid fixation obtained via titanium plates and screws.

Fixation between maxillary and mandibular teeth removed and intermediate splint discarded.

Mandibular bi-lateral osteotomy surgery:

Right posterior mandibular soft tissues injected for hemostasis.

Muco-periosteal incision slightly lateral to and along leading edge of ramus and into buccal sulcus.

Muco-periosteal flap reflected exposing lateral mandibular ramus and posterior body wall.

Medial reflection of surgical flap exposing ramus for

identification of sigmoid notch, posterior border and mandibula lingula

Channel retractor provided neurovascular bundle protection and adequate visualization.

Horizontal osteotomy through full width of ramus above lingula performed through inter-ramus bony cortex.

Vertical osteotomy performed adjacent to 2nd molar tooth and through lateral cortex from inferior border to alveolar crest.

Connecting osteotomy performed between horizontal medial and vertical lateral osteotomies.

Sagittal-split separation by reciprocating saw and osteotome.

Surgical site packed with moist gauze.

Similar step-by-step procedure performed for left osteotomy.

Right surgical site pack was removed.

Horizontal mandible was mobilized and freely advanced.

Throat pack was removed and area suctioned dry.

Mandible was counter-rotated into desired post-op relationship using final occlusal splint.

All reference lines indicated maxilla and mandible were in desired post-surgical relationship.

Rigid skeletal fixation was established using circum-mandibular and zygomatic wires.

All mucosal surgical sites were sutured closed.

Patient was prepared for transfer to recovery room.

Pack count and blood loss was verified.

Nasal intubation tube, nasal gastric tube and Foley catheter remained in place.

Immediate post-surgery:

Vital signs, antibiotics, steroids, pain medication, fluid replacement and blood loss replacement orders were written.

Transfer from recovery room to ICU ordered

N-G tube treatment for gastric distress and rectal suppository medication ordered, p.r.n.

ICU:

Rigid skeletal fixation of jaws supports need for close nursing supervision first 24 hours.

Immediate post-surgical considerations:

Vital signs stability.

Fluid I-O

Rigid skeletal fixation is maintained.

No sign of infection.

Nausea control.

Gradual fluid intake.

Lucid and ambulatory.

Potential post-surgery complications:

Undesired post-surgery jaw relationship.

Failure of rigid fixation.

Paresthesia.

Infection.

Consultation from a qualified source p.r.n.

APPENDIX D

An Airplane Pilot's Checklist

Normal Procedures
Table of Contents
(modified)

Normal Procedures Checklist	Normal Climb
Pre-Flight Inspection	Maximum Performance Climb
Before Starting Engine	Cruise
Starting Engine	Descent
Before Taxiing	Before Landing
Taxiing Normal	Landing
Before Takeoff	Short Field Landing
Takeoffs After	Landing
Normal Takeoff	Shutdown

Each of those listed headings top an individual list of steps each pilot should meticulously go through before and during each flight. Unfortunately, periodic newspaper articles illustrate how too many pilots become far too comfortable with their own ability to fly an airplane and end up paying a price for their personal lapse in judgment.

There is an uncanny similarity between flying a single-engine airplane and performing surgery, and I speak from experience of both. Those who seek to use the airline industry for innovative methods of greater patient safety *should* seek to use all of the best parts that industry uses on a daily basis.

Surgeon's Checklist

Patient's Medical Record

Initial Consultation	Pre-op Preparation
Chief Complaint	Anesthesia
Current and Past Medical History	Prepared for Surgery Patient
Differential Diagnosis (if needed)	Initial Surgical Access
Diagnosis	Surgical Correction
Treatment Plan	Response to Surgical Unknowns
Laboratory, x-rays, etc.	Surgical Closure
Informed Consent	Immediate Post-op
Scheduled for Surgery	Recovery

Earlier it was suggested that all physicians could benefit from taking a few lessons in how to fly a single-engine airplane, but only if they would attempt to compare the *science* and the *art* of each endeavor.

Military aircraft utilize a Form 1 and at the immediate end of every flight each crew-member is required to notify the pilot of any maintenance discrepancy to be noted for inspection. Thus, real-time notification of existing aircraft deficiencies are rapidly confronted.

Unrecorded operative mishaps have long been *best kept secrets* within every hospital medical staff in America. In reality, those *best kept secrets* are rarely secrets at all. Anesthesiologist, scrub and circulating nurses and others are the most likely individuals to be fully aware when surgical mishaps occur.

Every hospital medical staff in America should initiate a policy that the patient's medical record cover will have a red sticker attached when a surgical mishap occurs. Rapid, detailed follow-up should then take place in response to each such emergency classification.

Military and commercial aircraft industries have long had much to offer in the quest for greater patient safety within our health care system. Appendix D will take this concept one step further.

END NOTES

1   Paul Star, *The Social Transformation of American Medicine* (New York, Basic Books, 1982), 111–112.

2   Dr. John Clough, Editor, "Cleveland Clinic Journal of Medicine," Editorial May, 1997. National Quality Forum, www.qualityforum.org.

3   Shakespeare, Macbeth, Act 5 Scene 5